I'M A PARENT...
GET ME OUT
OF HERE!

Before I Kill
My Teenager!

By Darren Curtis

Absolutely Fabulous

British Library Cataloguing in Publication Data
A record for this book is available from the British Library.

ISBN-13: 978-0-9574604-0-9

Typeset by Juicy Marketing, Basingstoke, Hampshire, England.

Printed and bound in Great Britain by MPG Biddles Ltd

The paper and board used in this paperback are natural recyclable
products made from wood grown in sustainable forests.
The manufacturing processes conform to the environmental
regulations of the country of origin.

Absolutely Fabulous Ltd
25 Westwood Road,
Reading, RG31 5PL.

Acknowledgements

It seems hard to believe that I started scribbling my thoughts and stories onto paper some four years ago this very week whilst working in San Diego, so it seems fitting that I am writing the final part of this book in San Diego whilst on vacation.

The easiest and most obvious thank you is to my wife Tracy,

I am so grateful for the time, space and support given to me since I embarked on writing this book. When I have been away writing she has taken care of things back home, allowing me to relax and get creative, she's been supportive and above all, believed in me and what I am trying to achieve, to my darling wife, thank you, thank you, thank you.

A huge thank you must go to my teenage boys, Danny and Bailey, you are my inspiration, thank you for keeping me grounded and feeling younger than the birthdate printed on my passport would have you believe. I am so proud of you both for just being yourselves.

Thank you to Diane Dykes and her team at Juicy marketing for taking what was in my head and making it something attractive and easy to read, also for the many, many meetings, we'll get that sorted attitude and regular kicks up the bum for me to meet the deadlines on the way to creating this book! The journey has been so much more pleasurable spending it with you.

Thank you to my brother Colin for letting me use his home in the Highlands of Scotland when I needed to get away to gather my thoughts and for spending the time to read through and constructively comment on the chapters.

Thank you to my late father and my mum for loving me unconditionally throughout my childhood and helping me to grow into a happy, confident adult. Special thanks to my dad for helping me to always remember "you gotta have a laugh boy", a truly wonderful voice to have inside my head, thank you, thank you, thank you.

Thank you to my sisters, Jackie and Cindy for always being there, your sisterly love is very appreciated, I love you both very much, thank you, thank you, thank you.

Thank you to my father in law John for helping to keep my businesses running whilst I'm away and to Julie for keeping John grounded. Thank you to my mother-in-law Angela for all that you have done for me, Tracy and the boys, you are a very special lady, thank you, thank you, thank you.

Thank you to Lauren Miller and Fiona Cox for reading though the early drafts of this book and for the wonderful feedback, thank you, thank you, thank you.

Thank you to my nieces, nephews, aunties, uncles and cousins, for your time, your stories, your jokes, your laughter and your support, thank you, thank you, thank you.

Thank you to my main mentor through this process, Peter Thomson and the team at Peter Thomson International for your wisdom and direction, it has been and continues to be very much appreciated, thank you, thank you, thank you.

Thank you to Ian McDermott and Tim Hallbom and all the team at International Training Seminars for your clear, interesting and fun NLP and hypnosis training, thank you, thank you, thank you.

Thanks to Tom Evans, "the bookwright" for helping me to kick start the whole process of writing a book, thank you, thank you, thank you.

Thanks to Rose Moloney for providing me with a comfortable environment to write during my stay at Findhorn in the Highlands of Scotland, thank you, thank you, thank you.

Thank you to all my teachers who made learning fun and interesting and a special thank you to the teachers who made me feel like an idiot (and I mean that most sincerely) because without you, I wouldn't have such a strong desire to help teenagers as I do today and this book would not have been written, so thank you, thank you, thank you.

Thank you to my good friend Kim Wilson for being one of my spiritual compasses, you are a wonderful example to the world of a down to earth, positive, caring and encouraging parent, thank you, thank you, thank you.

Thank you to Simon Clarke for your faith and good humour, you are a true and loyal friend, thank you, thank you, thank you.

Thank you to Peter O'Mahony for having enough faith in my abilities as an author to be the first person to pre-order a copy of this book, thank you, thank you, thank you.

Thank you to all my coaching clients who place their trust in me to help them reach their goals, thank you, thank you, thank you.

Many, many thanks go to all the team, speakers, coaches, youth coaches and anyone who has ever attended the Anthony Robbins Foundation, global youth leadership summit (too numerous to mention, but you know who you all are) your energy and commitment is inspiring, I learn much more than I can ever teach whenever I spend time with you all, thank you, thank you, thank you.

And no thanks would be complete without thanking two very special people, firstly thank you so much to Davina Rasmussen, my first life coach, who opened my eyes to a completely new way of thinking and being. Your presence in my life all those years ago has had a profound effect on the direction of not only my life, but that of my wife's, my children and everyone I have gone on to work with. You are truly a spark that lit a flame within me, thank you, thank you, thank you. Also thank you Davina for introducing me to Anthony Robbins, for it is a combination of what you and Tony initially taught me, which has formed the foundation of the book you hold in your hands. Thank you Tony for all that you have done and continue to do, you are a very special man.

Finally, thank you to you the reader for having enough faith in me as an author to read this book from beginning to end and start to make the tiny changes necessary in your life to become more connected with yourself and your loved ones, I honour you, thank you, thank you, thank you.

Important

This book is not intended as a substitute for the medical advice of physicians. You should regularly consult a physician in matters relating to yours or your childs health and particularly with respect to any symptoms that may require diagnosis or medical attention.

Why me, why now?

Why me, why now?
Because I care and the time is right.

> *When I was 5 years old, my mother always told me that happiness was the key to life. When I went to school, they asked me what I wanted to be when I grew up. I wrote down 'happy'. They told me I didn't understand the assignment, and I told them they didn't understand life.*

John Lennon

To say I wasn't the most academic kid in school, is a gross understatement.

I guess I'm so passionate about the subject of teenagers and how to communicate more effectively with them, because I believe they are so often dismissed, undermined and misunderstood through no fault of their own. I'm aware that my last statement flies in the face of common thinking, but hey! following the herd was never really my thing and the following story may well give you a flavour of where my passion comes from.

I remember being in what is now referred to as the seventh year at school, when my English teacher asked me to stand up in front of the class and read from my book aloud. I was a reluctant reader with a belief back then that reading was boring (more about the affects of your beliefs later in the book) and I don't know about you? But reading from a book in front of my class mates was one of my least favourite things to do. After spending what seemed like a life time Er! Ah! and Um-ing! my way through the sentences, I'd barely completed a paragraph. When the teacher stopped me abruptly and with an undertone of sheer disappointment she bellowed "that was awful Darren. My seven year old daughter could do better than that. Sit down." I remember sitting down as fast as I could, my cheeks burning bright red with embarrassment, thinking, what a cow she was to embarrass me in front of my friends. I can sit here as an adult and ask myself, what possible good can my teacher have expected by speaking to one of her students like that? I didn't realise it at the time, but when I look back and understand I was one of the lucky ones, because my parents had let me know from as long back as I can remember, I could do anything I put my mind to and I was loved for being me, not the grades I achieved. From this I know I developed a supportive internal voice which says "it's ok, I'm ok and it'll be ok". So although this teachers comments did affect me with respect to crushing my desire to read even further, especially out loud! It didn't affect who I was as a person. But I know from working with thousands of teenagers over the years, that most of them do not have that supportive internal voice or a parent who thinks they're the greatest thing since sliced bread. They are usually full of doubt and negativity, with a parent or teachers voice in their head which says "who do you think you are?" "You'll never amount to anything" "You're as thick as two short planks", "I'm disappointed in you" or much, much worse. In fact, I was talking to a very articulate homeless guy on the streets of San Diego whilst writing some of the chapters for this book, who shared with me that he could still hear his late father's voice shouting at him "you're a bum, you'll always be a bum" Do you see the irony there? I'm sure his father didn't want or intend for his son to literally become a "bum", but your words as parents and teachers have the power to shape a youngsters decisions about what choices they make, what they choose to *do* or just as importantly, what *not* to do, the relationships they enter into and their relative fulfilment in life, "so no pressure there then, eh?"

In my eighth year at school, I had escaped from my previous English teacher only to be saddled with an equally venomous replacement (I'm sure she was a wonderful lady out of school?). When she was absent from school one week, we were asked to write a poem about war or destruction by our stand in teacher. This was my first experience of writing poetry and I throughly enjoyed it. We were asked to finish off the poem for homework and hand it in to our usual English teacher the following lesson. I proudly handed in my poem, knowing I had produced something quite special, only to be met with the words "are you sure this is your own work Darren, it seems far too good for you?" *There's nothing like a bit of encouragement is there?*

Those examples are from my schooling in the late 1970's/Early 80's and obviously things have come along considerably since then haven't they? Well in some ways yes, but my own son went through a period with a teacher who seemed to have very little emotional intelligence. When he was in primary school she would call him to the front of the class and shout "Bailey you are irresponsible", surely he'd misheard her, surely a teacher wouldn't attack an Eight year olds identity, would they? Nowadays every teacher is taught the importance of disciplining a child's behaviour, *not* their identity (if you're not already aware of the importance of this fact, more will be revealed as you continue reading), but it would seem that some teachers still ignore that vital piece of learning and choose instead to continue in their attempts to implant negative self beliefs into a child's head. Luckily my son knew this was wrong, which is why he bought it to my attention. He admitted what he'd <u>done</u> was probably irresponsible, but thankfully he knows that <u>he</u> is not an irresponsible child because he has grown up hearing his mother and I talking about the psychology behind identity v's behaviour.

To every parent whose child is coming up to or is already a pre-teen or teenager, then this book is written especially for you. Because I know a lot of what you are currently doing isn't working for you or your child and it's causing you and them some major stress. My original idea was to write something for my own teenage boys to assist their journeys into adulthood, but on chatting to them they seem pretty ok with most things. So I got to thinking about all the other parents I see who are stressed and struggling through their child's teenage years, most of which seems totally unnecessary. So this book has been written to piece together all the little gems which I've discovered through working with secondary/high school aged youngsters around the globe and an attempt to simplify and share the tools, techniques and actions necessary to create or recreate an effective communication channel between you and your children.

I'm also aware of how frustrating it can be for teachers of older children and I truly admire some of the work you do. However, I have to say, some teachers I've met and experienced really don't do themselves many favours. You probably know one or two? Maybe you could politely suggest they read this book? (if you're a teacher, who's colleague has politely suggested you read this book, welcome and enjoy the ride. You're gonna love it). Apologies in advance to any English teachers, I've probably made the odd punctuation and grammatical error and to be honest I'm actually not that fussed, because this book is about helping you to make tiny shifts in your psychology to help you and the children you interact with. It's not about being grammatically correct.

I also think the time is right to change the age old perception that somehow the majority of teenagers are monsters. We can learn just as much from our teenagers as we can ever hope to teach them. The trick is to actually shut up and listen sometimes, something we often preach to our children, but often conveniently forget to do ourselves.

Every day I hear parents who are constantly moaning about their children, especially their teen or pre-teen. But I'm also aware, even with all the knowledge my wife and I have accumulated in this field, how wrong we sometimes get it when we are under pressure and emotions are running high. It's knowing what to do to make things better after an argument or the words to avoid using during an argument that help so much to ensure all of our relationships remain healthy and positive.

It is my intention that this book is an aid for parents and teachers who'd like to take responsibility to communicate and connect more effectively with their children. It not only helps you get more of what you want out of life, ensuring you are happy with who you are and the choices you make, but also adds to the enrichment of all your relationships and isn't that what we all want for ourselves and our children?

" *The illiterate of the 21st century will not be those who cannot read and write, but those who cannot learn, unlearn, and relearn.*

Alwin Toffler

Chapter

Mind your language

Why is it whenever most people see a sign that says "wet paint, do not touch", they have to go and touch it?

Or at least get the urge to touch it, just to check. It's the same wall or door frame they have walked past without touching for many years, but as soon as the sign instructs them "do not touch", they feel compelled to touch it.

Most parents and teachers I speak to know what they don't want. They don't want their kids to be naughty, they don't want them to be disrespectful, they don't want them to get in with the wrong crowd and they don't want them to be late for class or to come home late. Unfortunately our subconscious mind doesn't recognise the difference between a positive or a negative instruction. Let me share some interesting facts with you which will help clarify the previous statement.

We are all susceptible to other's suggestion's. When you communicate with your children you are attempting to persuade them to do certain things in certain ways. When you watch a television advert, the company is suggesting (trying to persuade) you to choose their product over their competitors. Hypnosis is based on the power of suggestion and as a certified hypnotist I can assure you that it's just as easy for someone to hypnotise themselves or others about what they don't want, as it is to hypnotise them regarding what they do want.

Not sure what I'm talking about? Try this exercise. Whatever happens, please do not think of a pink cat, so just to be crystal clear about this, you can think of anything except a pink cat.

Are you thinking of a pink cat, when I specifically asked you not to?

In fact, you probably have never thought of a pink cat until the moment I asked you not to think of one. Unless of course you're a big fan of Bag puss (The BBC children's series about a saggy pink cloth cat) or the Cheshire cat from *Alice in Wonderland.* I must confess to being a fan of both. Even if you say you weren't thinking of a pink cat consciously, your subconscious mind had to create a picture of one, for you to know what I was asking you not to think of. How strange is that? Bizarrely enough, you may now even think of a pink cat before you go to bed tonight or even dream about one, just because I asked you not to think of one and that my friend holds the power to where we send our own or our children's focus.

So where might you be guilty of telling your children to focus on what you don't want?

"Don't answer me back!"
"Don't speak to me like that!"
"Don't be home late!"
"Don't be so disrespectful!"
"Don't leave your homework until the last minute!"
"Don't forget your keys!"

Do these requests sound like things you might say in an attempt to maintain control of a situation?

May I be so bold as to ask you, how well is that working for you? Not so good, I would guess, because this is your equivalent of the big pink cat!!!

Let's just remove the word *don't* from all of the aforementioned requests and see what you're actually programming or hypnotising them to do.

"*Answer me back*"
"*Speak to me like that*"
"*Be home late*"
"*Be so disrespectful*"
"*Leave your homework until the last minute*"
"*Forget your keys*"

Exactly what you don't want!!! Crazy, but true. I'm sure you can add another dozen well used negative requests/phrases to the list which you regularly bark at your children.

Examples of a more positive way to request what you actually do want would be;

"I need you to listen"
"Please speak to me with some respect"
"Please be home on time" or "please be home before 9pm"
"Please do your homework on time"
"Please remember your keys"

Perhaps you may be reading this book because you have a problem or challenge with your child. So my question to you is: "What exactly do you want from your child?"

I know you may think you don't know what you want, because like many other parents and teachers I work with, you're stuck in a rut and find yourself saying the same things over and over again, getting the same result or lack of results. I call this the "*fly at the window*" syndrome.

Have you ever seen a fly bouncing off the window pane?

What does the fly actually want? It wants to find a way out, freedom, right? But it keeps hitting the same window pane over and over again. And no matter how many times the fly does this, each time it expects a different result and we all know that ain't gonna happen. So you either squash him or if you're like me, you open the nearest window to let him out.

But what does the little fella do? Does he take the hint and fly straight out the open window or does he usually carry on bouncing off the same window pane, even though the escape route is only inches or centimetres away? Even when I gently encourage him in the general direction of the open window to freedom, he keeps banging his head against the same window pane, expecting a different result?

Well the good news is, the solution to your problem or challenge is closer than you think when you choose to stop banging your head against the same window pane and I encourage you to take it.

To demonstrate the power of the subconscious programming you and I do all the time, and how we get what we *don't* ask for (i.e what we ask for in a negative way), you may be interested in the following two stories.

For some reason best known to the carpet cleaning pixies, the majority of drinks I would give to my children when they were young would be spilt, despite my continuous requests for them to "please don't spill it". I was painfully aware that what I was currently doing wasn't working, something had to change and so the experiment commenced. I handed them each a plastic cup half filled with juice, telling them "please *don't* spill it", stepped back and watched them without their knowledge. They would take a sip, then place the half full cups on the carpet next to where they were playing. Six minutes and 37 seconds later Danny swung his leg round and over the cup went. Imagine as before, taking the word "don't" out of the equation. I was basically giving them the request or suggestion to "please spill the drink" and they dually obliged.

What was it I actually wanted them to do? I wanted them to *be careful*. And so I changed my strategy and asked them to "*Please be careful with the drink*" as I handed the drinks to them later the same day. Now I'd told them what I wanted, I would once again step back and observe them without their knowledge. To my surprise, I watched them place the cup of juice on the small table next to the sofa, play for a while, take a slurp, go back to play and repeat this until the drink was all gone (into their bellies rather than onto the carpet!). Just to be sure this wasn't a fluke, I reverted back to my old negatively framed request of "Don't spill the drink" and more often than not it would end up on the carpet again. When I asked them to "please be careful with the drink", it never got spilt.

Since then I have helped hundreds of parents to re-phrase their requests from what they don't want to what they do want, with incredible results.

Some years ago I worked with a wealthy family who's son seemed to be going off the rails, hanging around with the wrong crowd and generally not doing what he was told. After some initial conversations it became clear that the father of this fifteen year old boy was constantly pointing out the pitfalls of mixing with the wrong crowd and he shared with me the conversations he'd had with his son from an early age with regards to the "rough" family who lived down in the village. As he would drive past the "rough" family's house he would point and say to his son, "I'd better not catch you mixing with Jack's son". Can you see how he was drawing attention to the very person he didn't want his son to be spending time with and if we look at the hypnotic language behind the last sentence, he was basically telling his son "I'd better ~~not~~ catch you mixing with Jack's son". Jack's son had become the pink cat. Guess who he was spending most of his time with as he got older?

Yep! Jack's son.

Another great example of the changes which take place when you choose to ask for what you want was when a mother called me to ask for help with her fifteen year old daughter. Who in her opinion was hanging around with the wrong crowd, staying out late and generally doing a lot less than she was capable of at school (sound familiar?)

After her daughter had gone out at the end of the second coaching session, I asked the mum, "out of all the battles you're currently trying to fight, how many are you winning?"

"Now let me see" she said, "There's the untidy room battle, the staying out late battle, the hanging around with the wrong crowd battle and the doing poorly at school battle, mmmm! None."
she sighed.

"So if you had to choose one battle to win, which one would it be?" I asked.

I needed her to get clear on what was most important to her, because as things were at the moment, she just seemed to be moaning at her daughter whatever she did and all her daughter could hear was a constant nagging, moaning, drone and something needed to change.

"I'd want her to stop coming home late" was her reply and as if just to confirm to her self she repeated "The battle I'd want to win, is for her to stop coming home late"

Now this is an excellent example of a parent focussing on what they *don't* want. She doesn't want her daughter coming home late.

So I asked, "what do you say before you daughter leaves the house in the evening?"

She replied with a puzzled look on her face, "I tell her, she's not to come home late, in fact I tell her to be home no later than 10:00pm"

I also found out that she would often tell her daughter that she was sick of her always being late and treating their home like a hotel. So if I take those last couple of statements first, this mum is telling her daughter what she doesn't want and she is telling her that she treats the home like a hotel. I have two teenage boys and I know that emotions can run high and we sometimes say things that we don't mean, but these kinds of statements only serve to make matters worse. She is effectively hypnotising her daughter to do what she doesn't want her to do. Why would you do that? Well we can only presume that it is a lack of knowledge in this area.

If you were aware of a different way of communicating, which was proven to work, you'd use it wouldn't you? In fact by the end of this chapter, it'd be great if you were able to say to yourself "I'll handle these situations in a more positive and assertive manner."

Back to the story.

What did she actually want? It took a few attempts, but we finally got to the fact that she wanted her daughter to "come home *before* 10pm". Why? "because we love her and it means her father and I can relax and go to bed at a reasonable hour knowing she's home safely"

I then asked "next time she goes out with her friends, I want you to tell her what you've just told me"

"but she'll think I'm taking the Mickey" was the reply.

"Just do it and see what happens" I insisted.

The following Monday I received a phone call from a very excited mum, who started the conversation with "It can't be that easy, otherwise everyone would do it"

"Do what?" I questioned.

"As my daughter was leaving the house on Friday at 6pm to go out with her friends, I said to her, please be home *before* 10pm, because you know your father and I love you very much and it means we can relax and go to bed at a reasonable time. And you'll never guess what happened - she came home at 9.45pm, fifteen minutes early, that's the first time in the past six months that she's done what she's been told"

13

But I would put it to you, as I did to her on that Monday phone call. You've rarely been telling her what you wanted; only what you didn't want and either way, she gave it to you.

Your life and your relationships will transform when you choose to focus on and ask for what you want, instead of asking for what you don't want. A seemingly small but absolutely vital change in your language. It may take some practice, especially if you're entrenched in doing it the old way, the fly at the window way, the way that doesn't work.

So just to clarify, I'm suggesting you start to practice the art of focussing and asking for what you want and I look forward to you emailing me your positive stories.

I'd like you to carry on reading this book!

Chapter

Worrying about an if...

Worrying about an if...

A lot of teenagers and pre-teens who are referred to me, worry about stuff that might happen in the future or has happened in the past (or at least their version of it has happened in the past). They worry about things like starting school or a new job, commenting "What if I can't do it?" or "What if I don't know what I'm doing?" They worry about exams, stating "What if I don't get the results or grades that I need?" and then there's the social side of things, "What if they don't like me?" or "What if I end up on my own at lunchtime?"

These are all what I refer to as "a *negative* what if" statement. Because these youngsters are spending a significant amount of time and energy worrying about an event or situation that may not and probably will not happen. But they have taken the time and effort to go through the various negative scenarios, even taking the time to worry about the smallest detail, as if it were already reality. Some youngsters are especially good at doing this and literally worry themselves sick.

One such example was a young girl I was working with called Rachel. Her mum had called me to say that Rachel was really nervous to the point of nearly being physically sick and she was worried that she would have to miss her first day at secondary school. When I arrived, Rachel was curled up on the sofa, her knees were tucked up under her chin, her head was down and it was clear that she'd been crying.

"Fancy a chat?" I said, "not really" she replied solemnly, because, of course, that's what eleven year old girls do!

"Your mum said you were worried about starting your new school tomorrow? I continued, "so what are you thinking?"

She thought for a while, then replied, "What happens if I get split up from my friend?"

Before I could reply, she continued, "What if the teachers don't like me or the lessons are too hard or even worse I'll probably get lost, because the school is massive?"

Once again I tried to reply, but stopped, sensing Rachel had some more to say (not bad for someone who initially didn't want to talk!)

This time she took a deep breath to enable her Olympic attempt at another sentence, "I probably won't like any of the food at lunchtime and I've heard they bully the new kids if they don't like you and what if I'm forced to sit next to someone I don't like and did I mention that I'm really worried about getting lost?"

I paused for a second before replying, "Those are all valid worries Rachel, however, from the look of you, all these things have already happened."

"I feel sick." She replied.

I handed Rachel a black sheet of A4 paper and some coloured pens, "write down exactly how you'd like your first day at school to go, from the moment you get up in the morning, in fact write it down as if it happened yesterday."

This is what she wrote;

"I woke up yesterday at 6am, excited that it was my first day at secondary school, mum was calm and dad had arranged to go to work later so he could be there for me in the morning. My hair looked nice and mum drove me to school with plenty of time to spare. We picked up Stacey on the way so we could arrive together. We were met by a nice teacher, who gave us a map of the school and showed us where to go. We were shown to our new class room and my form tutor was really helpful and fun. We played games and I got to know the other kids. I have a great class and made lots of new friends, lunch was nice and everyone was helpful and friendly. Mum was waiting for me in the car park after school. I called my coach and told him that the whole day had gone much better than I guessed it would be."

She smiled when she'd finished writing the letter and said, "but it might not happen like this."

"But what if it does? How great would that be?" I replied.

If Rachel was your child, you can see from what she has written, some of the things that will help her to stay *calm*, like getting up early to give her the time to get ready and look nice. Both mum and dad are there to *support* her before school, she also wants the *support* of her friend Stacey on the way to school and finally mum there to *support* her again at the end of the day. By knowing all of this, it is easier to put these things into place to create a *supportive* environment for Rachel and help *calm* her nerves. Obviously this is Rachel's version of a perfect first day, for another youngster, this would be their worst nightmare as they may prefer to walk to and from school with a couple of mates and the further their parents are from things the better. So each youngster should be treated differently according to what it is *they* actually want and need.

Back to Rachel's story, I asked her to focus on what she'd just written, a "*positive* what if", instead of the "*negative* what if" she'd previously been discussing. She agreed to focus on the "*positive* what if" story that made her smile and when she called me the next evening, she said "the whole day was much better than I guessed it would be, much more like the story she had written".

And isn't that often the case, especially during periods of change and uncertainty? You can sometimes spend so much time and energy worrying about something that *might* happen that you create a very negative picture of the future which is completely false. This is often referred to as False Expectations Appearing Real (FEAR). Whatever you are most fearful of almost certainly never actually happens. So what was the point of spending all that time and energy worrying about it in the first place?

Your time and energy is much better spent creating the future with a "positive what if" and the best thing of all is that it's actually easier to do, once you get a little practice.

So when you're next trying to help a child who is worrying about a "*negative*, what if". I'd like you to help them turn their focus towards the best possible outcome and focus on their own "*positive*, what if". The best kind of what if, "What if things turn out exactly how you'd like them too?"

Obviously, we don't know what the future may or may not hold for us and it is fine to plan for certain negative eventualities, but if that planning turns into panic and anxiety, I would strongly recommend you help the individual focus on the best possible outcome, giving them the time and space they need to create it and letting them use their own words.

If you're a teacher, try writing out your perfect day at school, from the time you wake up in the morning to the moment you go to bed. How are the kids at school? How are you feeling? What are you thinking about in your perfect day?

If you're a parent, what would a great home life be like? What time would you get up in the morning? Earlier or later? What time would the kids get up? Would they make their own breakfast or would you have breakfast as a family? How would your day play out? Would you be there for the kids when they got home from school? Would you like to have dinner together? if so, what time? What would you do differently in the evening?

Just write it out, be honest and be bold. You may even surprise yourself.

> *Our highest endeavour must be to develop individuals who are able out of their initiative to impart purpose and direction in their lives.*
>
> Rudolf Steiner

19

Take a few minutes to imagine and write down what your perfect day was like, remember to use positive language and past tense, as if it had already happened yesterday.

"My perfect day started yesterday when I…….."

Chapter

three

Motivation

Motivation

A positively framed goal has immense power for our minds to work towards. By positive I mean something along the lines of "I'd like to have healthy meals together as a family at least four times a week" rather than the negatively framed equivalent "I want the kids to have less take-aways in front of the television". As I've pointed out in the first chapter "Mind your language", the latter is focussing on the very thing you don't want and you are now more aware of how futile that can be – remember

the pink cat I asked you not to think about?

Goals are important, they give us and our children something to focus on, something to aim for. They engage the reticular activating system in the brain, which controls what we look for and what we notice. In it's simplest form, if you look for problems, you'll find them. If you look for solutions, you'll find them. So I urge you to shift your thinking from a problem solver to a solution seeker. They may *sound* like two sides of the same coin, but I can assure you the difference to your end result will be significant. I encourage all of my students to set what I call a dream goal, asking them "If anything were possible, what would you do, be or have?"

I remember working with a group of students in a school near my home town of Reading in England and one particular young man called Craig introduced himself to me as the naughtiest kid in the school. A label he wore with some pride. I later found out, he wasn't particularly good at sport and he was well below average academically, so he would never get recognition in those areas, therefore winning and gaining attention in the bad behaviour category was something he had found he could excel at!

During the dream goal exercise, I noticed Craig wasn't writing anything down and had started to doodle on his notepad and day dream. I respectfully asked him to share his dream goal with the class. After an initial pause and shrug of the shoulders, as if to say I don't know, he replied "I wanna be a millionaire". At this point a variety of pens, pencils and rubbers were launched across the room at Craig, accompanied by jeers from his class mates of "you can't even read and write properly, how are you gonna make a million pounds?"

I can imagine those were a good reflection of the internal voices that would plague someone like Craig into their adult years and stop them achieving such grand goals, especially if those internal voices remained unchecked. (Just to be clear, your internal voice is simply you talking to yourself, without speaking out loud. We all do it, it's ok. It'll become clearer in chapter 5)

Once the room was calmed, I asked Craig when he thought it was realistic to be a millionaire by? He sat up straight and declared that he'd like to be a millionaire by the time he was thirty years old. (Because obviously that's ancient, when you're only fourteen)

I asked Craig to imagine that it was his thirtieth birthday today and he was walking across his hallway to his front door to collect his mail. "What kind of front door do you have at your home now you're thirty?"

He puffed out his chest with pride and declared "Well, I built the house myself, so it's a solid oak door with brass fittings".

The class was surprisingly quiet at this point, I think they were in shock because Craig was actually going along with the scenario, instead of playing the fool.

I went on to ask another question "Amongst all your birthday cards is a letter from your bank containing your bank statement, as you pick it up and open it you are pleasantly surprised by the balance showing in the bottom right hand corner. It says you are One Million Pounds in credit. Congratulations you've achieved your goal. You are thirty years old and you have become a Millionaire. How does that make you feel?"

Craig took a deep breath, puffed out his chest once more and extended in height by at least six inches, before telling me it felt great.

"It's taken you sixteen years and one million pounds, so what has that really given to you personally Craig?"

He paused and thought before replying "It's gonna make my mum really proud..."

"That's excellent Craig. Just out of interest, what could you do this week to make your mum really proud?" I asked

Again he paused before replying "I suppose I could clean my bloody bedroom up" to which the whole class roared with laughter.

I confirmed with Craig when he would like to clean his bedroom by and he agreed that the coming weekend would be as good as any.

The following week, his mum stopped me at the school gates to ask what I'd done to her son. When I looked at her in a puzzled way, she continued to tell me that she'd been trying to get him to clean his room up for the past two years, with limited success, until suddenly last weekend he'd cleaned it to the highest of standards without prompting.

"Were you proud of him?" I asked

"Yes, of course" she replied

"Did you let him know you were proud of him?" I continued

"No, I just told him it was about bloody time and he'd better not be expecting any favours in return"

I shared with her the story I've just told you, about how he came to *want* to clean his room and with tears rolling down her face she mumbled "I didn't know".

"Please let your son know you're proud of him, because that's all he wants"

Because that's all any youngsters want, especially the "naughtiest kid" in the school. They want their parents and teachers to be proud of them and if they can't find something positive, to be great at a sport or excel in a certain subject, bizarre as it may sound, they will find something "bad" to be good at, because at least it gets your attention.

Craig was willing to wait sixteen years and amass a million pounds to make his mum proud, when there were much simpler, quicker ways to achieve the same goal and isn't that always the way?

So often we don't give our children a chance to dream, we try to be too

practical and realistic, presumably to protect them from being
disappointed? In the process we may be squashing our children's dreams
before they even get a chance to take root, only for them to lead a life of
mediocrity, reaching middle age and wondering "is this it?" Can you see
how important it is to let them express what they *think* they really want to
enable them to get to what's behind the goal and see what's *really* driving
them?

> ❝ *Never tell people how to do things.*
> *Tell them what to do and they*
> *will surprise you with their ingenuity.* ❞
>
> George S. Patton

Which areas of your life are *you* putting off until tomorrow, that could easily be achieved today?

Chapter

What's important to you

v's

What's important to them

What's important to you v's What's important to them

Core values

I like to play a little game with the teenagers I work with. The game has only one rule and the rule is "you can't start until the other person has started." I usually have to repeat this one simple rule a couple of times as my students try and work it out. With a puzzled look on their faces, they exclaim, "but that makes no sense", if I can't start until somebody else has started and they can't start until I start, then the game will never begin?"

"But surely this is a game you play every day" I reply.

The puzzled looks continue, until I explain further.

"I'm not saying sorry, until they say sorry or they don't respect me, so why should I show them any respect?". Then I ask them to think of other examples of where in their life this rule keeps showing up?

The result of asking this question to thousands of teenagers has led me to the conclusion that dishonouring the values of Respect, Freedom, Fairness and Support seem to be the trigger for many arguments or perceived "bad behaviour".

Each of us has our own set of values. These are what determine which aspects of life we regard as important to us as individuals. Our values help determine what we will spend our time doing, how we spend our money, what hobbies and social activities we pursue. We each hold many values and our top values are referred to as our core values, as they are at the core of what we stand for. When you give them an order of importance, this will help you to understand your own and your child's decision making process and motivators.

Often, home and school can become a place of conflict if the values of a teacher do not align with the values of the student. (I.e. a teacher who insists "you're *not* here to have fun you know" is going to have a hard time understanding the motivations of a student whose highest value is fun!) Similarly, a parent who has a high value of order and organisation will have a hard time understanding a child whose core values are connection and creativity, especially when they drop everything to connect with their friends and their creative ways of doing homework involves mess and disorder. In fact, it is our individual values which contribute to motivating us to take action or cause us to procrastinate. There are no correct values or better values, because each value will have a unique meaning to each individual. Rather than creating conflict by insisting that our values are correct and trying to impose them onto our children, a more sensible thing for you and I to do is to live our values daily, enabling our children to understand what is important to us through our actions. However, if you would like to achieve a greater understanding of what makes your child tick and how to get the best out of them, taking the time to discover what your children's values are and learning to work with them to keep them motivated is your key to success.

Generally teenagers will give respect once they feel it has been given to them and this can cause a significant friction to the third parties involved. However, I've noticed a lot of adults, (especially teachers and parents) seem to play by the same rules in thinking they are somehow due respect as a pre-requisite of their position or status. From my experience, I have found that by simply showing respect first, it is always reciprocated, even by the most challenging of youngsters, maybe not immediately but it always follows pretty quickly. Think about it for a second, I'm sure you'll have a value of respect at some level, most people have. In the pursuit of ensuring that value is honoured, you may make the mistake of thinking respect is something that is done to you or you insist on receiving. Whereas, I would suggest it is much more useful to view something we value, in this instance "respect" as a triangle, with one side reflecting how much respect you are shown by others, the second side is how much respect you show to others and the third side is how much respect you have for yourself.

" One has to disrespect oneself to enable others to disrespect them. "

Unknown

29

Please take a minute to complete the following exercise;

On a scale of 0 to 10 (zero being "not at all" and 10 being "all the time"). How much self respect do you have?

On a scale of 0 -10, how much respect do you show to your children/students?

On a scale of 0 -10, how much respect do you get from your children/students?

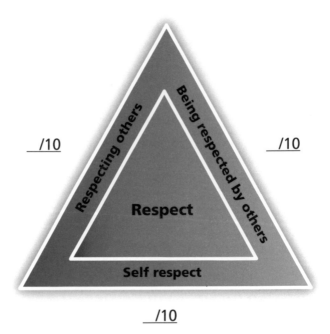

If I were a betting man, I would bet that the higher your scores were for your first two answers, the higher degree of respect you are currently enjoying from others.

Somewhere, in a land far away, there was a temple that housed a hall of a thousand mirrors. One day it so happened that a dog got lost in the temple and arrived at this hall. When the dog saw the reflections he showed his teeth and growled and a thousand dogs showed their teeth and growled back. The dog was furious that he was not being shown more respect, so he growled even deeper and barked his most fierce bark and one thousand dogs, growled even deeper and barked more fiercely straight back. With this the dog turned and ran with his tail between his legs, thinking that he would never return to such a hostile place ever again.

Sometime later, another dog was similarly lost in the temple. This time, however, when he saw one thousand reflections, he panted and wagged his tail with joy and a thousand dogs, panted and wagged their tails back at him. He barked a playful bark and a thousand dogs, barked a playful bark right back. The dog left with a smile on his face thinking "What a friendly place, I must come back here often."

You cannot change the level of respect others give you by demanding respect, but you can easily increase your self-respect and the respect you show to others. Therefore if you scored lower than you'd have liked on the previous exercise, take some time now to write out what you can start doing today to show more respect to yourself and others.

I was working with a young man in a school in the southern counties of England, who was deemed by his teachers as having anger management issues. During one of our early sessions we carried out a values elicitation and found his five core values to be freedom, capability, support, respect and fun. I asked him to explain the sequence of events leading up to his last outburst in class. He told me that he'd been made to feel stupid by his teacher in front of the class. He saw red, swore at the teacher, threw a chair into the wall and stormed out of the classroom.

> *When our core values are being dishonoured, we will often resort to uncontrollable extremes of emotion.*
>
> Darren Curtis (Author)

I asked him what value was being dishonoured to make him react in such an extreme way "I guess I felt unsupported and disrespected". It's important to remember here, that any extreme reaction is a result of our values being perceived to be dishonoured. I say perceived, because we all have our own set of rules which tell us when a value is being honoured or dishonoured.

So someone with a rule that says, I will only be happy when everyone respects me, is going to be unhappy on a regular basis, because what are the chances of everyone respecting you all of the time? It just ain't gonna happen. So it's easier if you become aware of these rules and help yourself or the youngster to change them to make them easy to achieve, (i.e. "I always feel respected whenever I show others respect" would be easier to achieve because it's something you are in control of).

I then asked him, "which of your values was being honoured by acting the way you did?"

His first reply was "Surely, none of my values were being honoured, I wasn't proud of my behaviour, I wasn't supporting the class or the teacher, it wasn't fun and I certainly wasn't showing any respect?"

"But you were honouring at least one of your values" I continued.

He thought some more, before answering slowly, as if he'd just uncovered a hidden truth,

"I guess I could have been honouring my value of freedom, because I ended up getting out of the class?"

I questioned further, "So exactly how much freedom did you get?"

His reply "I got about two minutes of freedom when I initially stormed out of the class, then I was sent to the deputy heads office, my parents were called and I was sent home, then grounded for the rest of the week"

Now isn't that interesting, how this young man's subconscious mind found a very effective way of getting out of any of his classes where he didn't feel capable or supported. Especially as the ultimate punishment was to be sent home to potentially more freedom (depending on his parents rules on punishment). And let's face it, even sitting in your bedroom can *feel* like freedom, if you dislike certain teachers or lessons. Just like our subconscious mind will try to keep us safe and make us feel sick on the day when we're due to do a big talk or something we don't feel confident with (remember Rachel's first day at secondary school - literally worrying herself sick. For the record, some of Rachel's core values were Safety, Support and Fun).

This young man's unconscious mind had found a way to get him "freedom", which would also explain why he said he didn't feel he was in control during the event and he felt really guilty afterwards.

I do what I do and asked another question, "What could you do next time you get angry to ensure you honour your values of respect AND freedom?"

I allowed him the time and space he needed to answer such a question and he eventually replied, "when I get that tight feeling in my stomach, just before I see red, I could just walk out of the class, without disrespecting the teacher or myself". Then almost immediately he added, "but that won't work, because I'll still get into trouble for leaving the class"

"So what else needs to happen to make it work?" I asked.

Once again there was silence while he thought long and hard, before replying, "I could tell the deputy head the stuff I've just learned and ask her permission to be excused from class for five or ten minutes whenever I see red. That way, all the teachers will know what I'm doing and I can return to class once I've calmed down and it's better for everyone". Before he'd even finished the sentence, once again he answered himself, "but, she'll never agree to that".

My reply "what have you got to lose?"

That afternoon, he went to the deputy head as agreed, put the proposition to her. She agreed to a short trial on the condition that he went to a certain room to cool down where a support teacher helped other children with academic challenges (by happy coincidence, this honoured his value of support). He agreed, the trial period was made permanent and I understand that it was rolled out to other pupils with similar issues in school.

Another trigger for your child's negative behaviour can be injustice or perceived injustice. The "problem" child turns up to class five minutes late or does something wrong and the teacher or parent is onto them like a wasp around an open cola can. But when the "A grade" child walks in five minutes late or does the same thing wrong, everything's fine, we let it go, why? Because really we're punishing the "problem" child for all the other stuff we've stacked up in our memory over time and there is a perceived amount of "disrespect" from them and hey! they're not being fair, so why should we be fair to them? (remember the game with one rule?). But wait a minute, there's no perceived "disrespect" from the "A grade" child ,Why? Because we haven't stacked emotions, they don't make a habit of it, name your excuse.

They haven't dishonoured one of your values, you don't believe they were disrespectful by being late and you're probably right. But the two children have done the same thing, haven't they? So many of my students give such examples of people or life not being fair. Remember, if they believe "life isn't fair", they'll create situations which prove them right? Our job is to help prove them wrong.

I laughed when I was chatting to a good friend of mine over dinner one night, when he recounted a story of how angry he'd got, because of the local youngsters having no respect. He went on to tell me that he was walking up a stepped alleyway with a handrail running up the middle. Two youngsters were talking half way up and their bikes were blocking his path, forcing him to cross under the handrail and walk on the opposite side of the alleyway. "Bloody teenagers, trying to provoke me, spoiling for an argument" he said.

Quite shocked, I replied "But how do you *know* that's what they were trying to do?"

"It's obvious, they'd have moved if they'd have been polite, one even said, alright mate? just to take the piss".

"Surely he realised what he'd done and was trying to make a connection" I explained

He barked back at me "No he wasn't, he was trying to provoke me, so I told him, I'm not your bloody mate!"

So I put it to my friend, "If two elderly gentlemen had met at the same place and were so deep in conversation that they hadn't noticed you, until you got right up to them and as you crossed under the handrail, one of them had said "alright mate?", would you still have replied, "I'm not your bloody mate"?

"Of course not..." he replied.

Different rules for different people who we perceive to be "A grade" or "A problem".

If you and I can master the balance of respect, freedom, support and fairness, the majority of the youngsters with perceived "problems" will respond positively.

" *Everyone is a genius, but if you judge a fish on its ability to climb a tree, it will live its whole life believing that it is stupid.* "

Albert Einstein

Chapter

Changing your internal voice - as simple as ABC

Changing your internal voice – as simple as ABC.

Many youngsters I talk to are self conscious and/or lack self esteem. Not necessarily all of the time, but definitely in certain situations, especially when they're unsure. Which, let's face it, whether you're six, sixteen or sixty years old, your confidence levels can take a dip whenever you're presented with a situation that you're unsure of. Often a child will have a nagging, doubting, whining voice inside their heads, which makes them very negative and either passive or aggressive, when I'm sure you'll agree, it's much better to be positive and assertive. In an attempt to keep things simple, I get them to ask themselves the following question;

"Am I my own best friend or my own biggest critic?"

Just stop and listen to what you're saying to yourself for a second...

I've heard it said, if you talk to yourself, you must be crazy? Well, if that were the case, then the men in white coats are going to be working overtime rounding us all up, because we all talk to ourselves, all of the time, whether you're aware of it or not is a completely different matter? Come on, you certainly don't say everything you think out loud, do you? You'd get in all sorts of trouble, wouldn't you? I know I would!

When you take the time to stop and listen to the thoughts you are thinking, you have a constant chatter going on inside your head, it's just most of the time you're so used to your internal dialogue, you don't take any notice of it. At least you don't take any notice consciously, but believe me; you're taking plenty of notice subconsciously.

What do I mean by that?

Imagine your internal voice is another person talking to you and just for a moment, take that voice outside of your head and notice what it would be like to have someone speak to you like you speak to yourself. Is it a friend whispering supportive words, cheering you on and encouraging you or is it a nagging, negative, whining critic who reminds you of past failures, points out your supposed faults, puts you down and generally holds you back?

> *the latter is often referred to as your gremlin -*
> *the annoying little $h!t£, who wants to put*
> *a spanner in the works.*

I would urge you to listen to how you speak to yourself for a few days and keep a note of what you say, in fact, I dare you to start to do this regularly throughout the day starting today. Review your comments at the end of each day to check how friendly or how critically you are talking to yourself. This is so important because it helps you to become aware of any negative thoughts and from that awareness *you can change your thinking*.

When you change your thinking you change your behaviour, and when you change your behaviour, those around you change theirs.

Once you've become aware, the good news is, you're in charge of what and how you speak to yourself and you can choose to change it at any time. You have to believe me, when I say this is the key to a happier, more fulfilling relationship with yourself and your child. It's the bridge between having self doubt and being self assured.

One young lady I worked with some years ago called Jordan, had what is commonly referred to as a negative self image and low self esteem. She didn't really like herself and by default, presumed others did not like her either. On the surface, she felt like this was something out of her control, something that was almost impossible to change because it was just who she was. And in her mind if she was, by some miracle able to change, she would have to find out what the problem was and fix it, prior to moving on.

In my experience that could not be further from the truth. I like to keep things simple and use an ABC methodology to change your internal voice quickly and easily. As mentioned before, the first thing to do is become Aware. This could be that you become aware of certain behaviours or aware that other people don't necessary agree with your way of thinking or aware that there is a solution. Then you must Break the pattern, by doing something differently.

And finally, Comfort yourself.

> " *If you always do what you've always done, you'll always get, what you always got.* "
>
> unknown origin

The simplest way I have found to do this with clients like Jordan is to ask them to imagine that we've found a lost little child (imagine a child of three to four years old) who she must look after for a while. But there are two rules that must be followed if we are to look after this little lost child in a caring and loving way.

The first rule is;

Whenever you are *Aware* of saying anything negative to yourself, you need to say that exact same thing to the child in your care and see how it makes you feel saying that same negative phrase to someone much smaller and much more vulnerable than yourself.

The second rule is;

If you don't like how it sounds saying that negative phrase to the child, *Break* the pattern by re-phrasing it immediately and repeat what you would really like to say to the child to help Comfort them. Once you are happy you have helped the child feel good about themself, then repeat that same comforting sentence/phrase back to yourself.

This may sound a bit long winded, but once you get used to it, you can do it in a matter of seconds.

Jordan agreed to the two rules and we spoke the following week.

She shared that one of the first negative thoughts that she'd been *Aware* of, was when she looked in the bathroom mirror the following morning and said to herself "You're so ugly, you may as well be dead", she imagined looking into the small childs eyes who I'd asked her to care for and repeated "You're so ugly, you may as well be dead". After that, she told me she'd burst into tears, as she could hardly believe that she could utter such horrible, spiteful, bullying words to a another person, let alone a small child.

She continued to share that she'd wiped the tears from her cheeks, re-phrased the statement to how she'd like to speak to the child and without a second thought and as if instinctively knowing how to make the little girl feel better, she said "You are so beautiful, I love you" and with that, she stared back at her own reflection in the mirror, looking straight into her own eyes and repeated to herself "You are so beautiful, I love you". Another tear welled up in the corners of her eyes, but these were tears of sheer joy and apparently tasted much sweeter than the bitter tears she was used to, as she confessed to feeling an unfamiliar sense of self assurance and self worth coming from inside.

After letting her enjoy the memory of the feeling and the taste of the sweetest tears for a while longer, I asked how it felt saying the first negative statement to the little child and she shared with me that she would never normally speak to a little child like that and it felt completely wrong.

I continued "so why did you choose to speak to yourself like that?" The answer was quite simple and straight forward, "I didn't know that I did speak to myself like that?" She had only just become *Aware*.

Jordan agreed to continue to do this exercise for a while longer, to enable her to become even more *Aware* of her internal self talk.

During our next conversation, she shared with me, what she had caught herself saying when all her friends were meeting up after school one day. It went something like this, "They don't want you tagging along. They only asked you because they feel sorry for you". She immediately stopped herself, imagined she was talking with the little child and repeated that thought/internal dialogue immediately. Once again she said it sounded and felt terrible saying it to the little child, she confirmed it felt like she was bullying them again. So if she feels like she's bullying the little child by repeating her own self talk, what's she been doing to herself all these years? Jordan immediately re-thought and rephrased what she would like to say to the child. "It'll be ok, just go and enjoy yourself". Wow! what a difference, Jordan went from bullying herself to being her own best friend and this my friend is the difference between someone you might refer to as having low self worth or very little confidence, to someone who has self worth and is more confident. It is quite simply how you talk to yourself.

When you choose to be your own best friend, talk to yourself positively, encourage and support yourself as a best friend would, you will become more confident and self assured. After all you are giving yourself assurance.

> *Self assurance is simplicity itself;*
> *it is the positive, comforting words we*
> *choose to use to reassure ourselves*
> *internally, which show up as*
> *confidence externally.*
>
> **Darren Curtis (Author)**

Can you see how it is not only your job as a parent or teacher to become Aware of your own self talk, Break any negative patterns and use Comforting words and tones to help you succeed, but also to install this same comforting voice inside your children's head's. Because yours is one of the voices that is already a part of their internal dialogue. So the second important thing you need to ask yourself, when thinking about the way you speak to your child is "Am I their best friend or their biggest critic?"

How do I currently talk to myself?

Complete the following sentence

Life is...

I am ...

If you answered positively, that's great. If you answered negatively, what would you *choose* to replace those beliefs with?

Life is...

I am ...

"When you change your thinking you change your behaviour, and when you change your behaviour, those around you change theirs."

Chapter

six

Is it true or not?

Is it true or not?

Have you ever heard of the placebo effect?

A placebo is a sugar coated pill containing no drug, which is given to a control section of patients to test the validity of a drug being tested. This enables the laboratory to compare the results of

a the people who were given the drug.
b the people given the placebo.
c the people given nothing at all.

It is scientifically accepted that a significant proportion of the patients taking the placebo will experience an improvement in their symptoms. The only explanation for this is the power of their mind, they *believe* they have been given the drug which will help their symptoms, therefore their symptoms improve.

It is also scientifically accepted throughout sports psychology that it is just as important (if not more so) to train the mind to be successful and achieve results. The most successful athletes and sports professionals spend time imagining their desired outcome in their mind as well as training their bodies to be physically prepared. If they didn't believe they could win, it is unlikely they would no matter how physically fit they were.

My first experience of this was when I was struggling to achieve anything better than third place in the 800 metre running event at school. My form tutor at the time was Mr Pritchard and he advised me to imagine how I would run the perfect race prior to training each morning and see myself crossing the line in first place and become attached to what the feeling of winning would feel like.

From experience, and on paper the two other guys had better times than me, so they were certainly favourites to win on the day. However, I had imagined beating these two guys every morning for the previous month, so in my mind I'd already done it, I'd already imagined winning, I'd already imagined the excitement of being the first to cross the winning line. On the day of the race I stood on the starting line in the position I'd imagined and ran the race exactly as I'd visualised, staying only inches behind my two main competitors as we went around the track, until we came to the final bend, overtaking them and sprinting for all I was worth on the final straight to win the race, not by a small amount, but by the significant margin I had visualised.

I trust you'll agree your mind is a very powerful tool and you can just as easily assist it to work for you as you can against you and with this knowledge you can help your children to create a powerful and positive subconscious mind for themselves.

Our minds work on two levels, consciously and subconsciously.

Psychological warning - do not read the next few paragraphs
unless you want to understand your child and yourself a little better.

The conscious mind is the part of your mind responsible for logic and reasoning. If I asked you about the sum of two plus two it's your conscious mind which is going to be used to add the two numbers together.

Your conscious mind also controls the actions you take with intention while being conscious. For example, when you decide to make any voluntary action like moving your arm or leg to make yourself more comfortable, you have consciously decided, you feel uncomfortable and by moving your arm or leg into a different position you will feel more comfortable, so this is done by the conscious mind.

Whenever you are aware of the thing you're doing you can be confident that you are doing it with your conscious mind. If there is a drink beside you and you decided to take a sip, all of this process will be taken by your conscious mind because you were 100% conscious while doing it.

The conscious part of your brain is also known to be the gate keeper for your mind. If someone tried to present you with a belief, criticise you or call you a name, you consciously filter according to you current belief system whether it is true or false before letting it in.

If for example, someone told you that you are "stupid", your conscious mind will filter this statement depending on your current belief system. If you *believe* you are stupid, the statement is allowed past the gatekeeper to support your existing belief "yes I am stupid, here's even more evidence, another person is confirming I'm stupid" **OR** if you currently believe you are clever, your gatekeeper will question the statement/criticism as being false and either completely disregard the information or push the onus of the mistaken statement/criticism back onto the person making the statement (i.e. "they are wrong"), supporting your current belief, "I am clever".

This is why you will often here me referring to the fact that *we are all trying to prove ourselves right* all of the time and we are trying to prove ourselves right based on a set of beliefs about ourselves, others and the world around us which may or may *not* be true.

What is the subconscious mind?

The subconscious mind is the part of your mind responsible for your involuntary actions. Your heart beats and breathing rate are controlled by your subconscious mind. If you become aware of your breathing, know that your conscious mind will take charge and you will start to consciously breath, (in fact, you may find that you just took a deep breath as I made you conscious of your breathing). Once you relax and forget about your breathing, your subconscious mind takes charge and you start to breath subconsciously again.

Your emotions are also controlled by your subconscious mind. Which is why you may sometimes feel afraid, anxious, angry or down without wanting to experience such a feeling.

Your subconscious mind is also the place where your memories and beliefs are stored. The majority of the challenges you or your child will be experiencing are as a result of one or more limiting beliefs stored subconsciously. We all have limiting beliefs, it's just that some are more limiting than others.

The good news is, they can be changed, but the first step to changing a limiting belief is to recognise it's existence. Many people will insist "life's not fair" or "I'm unlucky" then wonder why they can't succeed.

I have been studying psychology, Neuro Linguistic Programming (NLP) and hypnosis for many years and I came to the conclusion along time ago that most of the psychological challenges people face can be traced back to limiting beliefs!

Self confidence can be improved by changing your beliefs about your abilities, skills and identity.

Trust issues can be resolved by changing limiting beliefs that you acquired as a result of perceived injustice and/or being mistreated in your past.

Self image can be enhanced by removing the incorrect limiting belief you formed about your looks a long time ago.

The best way to change a limiting belief is to convince the conscious mind logically to accept that it is limiting, in effect questioning it's validity. Then create a more empowering belief to replace it. The trick is to start noticing and gathering evidence to support the new empowering belief, enabling it to pass the gatekeeper into the subconscious mind.

In order to achieve the personal growth for you and your child, the best thing you can do is to understand the combined power of how the conscious and the subconscious mind work together.

One of the best demonstrations is how emotions can be controlled.

Since the trigger for your emotions is subconscious it's difficult to stop them, but knowing that your thoughts (how you talk to yourself) are processed through your conscious mind and your thoughts are the primary trigger for your emotions, you can easily control your thoughts and in turn your emotions. You may want to read that last paragraph again!

> *The only difference between "I can" and "I cannot" is a "not" and you want to avoid "nots", because "nots" help you hold onto things, they don't help you to move forward.*

I'm conscious (excuse the pun), beliefs are quite a subject to attempt to cover in a chapter and I'm sure I could easily write a whole book on this one subject alone, but there are so many other subjects we need to cover to ensure you get the greatest benefit for you and your relationship with your children.

I love working with teenagers because they seem to be more accepting of new ideas. They absorb the information without necessarily having to make complete sense of it, which means they take action and because of this they get the quickest results. I trust the following story helps clarify and instil the information from this chapter into your subconscious mind more easily;

I was asked to work with a young boy called Carlos. His step mum was concerned he was extremely quiet, spent the majority of his time out with friends or in his room and very little time with the family. She had presumed that he may be resentful towards her because he'd been forced to move from his own home abroad, where his real mother lived with his younger brother or maybe he was jealous of the relationship she had with his father or was it that he just didn't like her as a person?

Obviously, we didn't know if any of the aforementioned beliefs/assumptions were true, but as this was her current perception of the situation, can you see how it might affect how she reacted with worry, frustration, anger or sadness. All of which are un-resourceful states of mind to be in.

I'm not a therapist or counsellor, so it's not my job to find the core to the problem and in my experience teenagers don't want things to get all heavy and serious. It's my job to help teenagers and parents to find the most simple and effective solutions and way forward. The only way to find out what was really going on in Carlos's head was to have a chat.

During the first session Carlos shared with me, that he found it impossible to talk to his step mum. So Carlos's *limiting* belief was "I find it impossible to talk to my step mum". When we hold a *limiting* belief about something or someone, we search for evidence to prove ourselves right. So in Carlos's case he would go straight to his room after school, go out with friends for as long as possible and basically spend as little time as possible with his step mum, therefore cementing his belief that he found it impossible to speak to her.

I asked whether he liked the fact that he found it impossible to speak to his step mum. His reply was quick and to the point, "No, of course not, but it's the truth". And this is a very valuable lesson to us all. Our own beliefs always seem to be the truth to us, because as I pointed out earlier, we spend our lives searching for evidence to prove to ourselves, that what we believe about our identity, life and other people is in fact true.

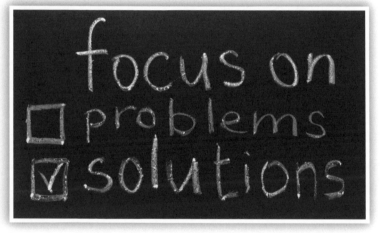

I went on to ask Carlos, "If I was to return in a couple of weeks and you could talk to your step mum, what might your new belief be?"

His reply after a little encouragement, "I suppose I would say something like, I find it easy to talk to my step mum"

I continued, "Ok, if you did find it easy to talk to your step mum, what sort of things would you do differently?"

Carlos initially looked down, before snapping his head up and answering, "Well, I know dad wants us to spend more time together as a family, so I guess I'd suggest we could all go to the cinema. That way, dad would be pleased because *I'd* made the suggestion, I'd feel more comfortable, because you don't need to talk while you're in the cinema and then we could chat about the film on the way home"

I don't know about you, but I thought that was a great solution and compromise?

I asked again "What else would you do as you find it easier to talk to your step mum?"

Carlos replied "Well, she's quite clever, so I guess I could ask her to help me with certain course work I'm struggling with"

I persisted in helping Carlos to find options by asking "What else?" over and over.

Carlos continued to build a picture of what life would be like *if* he found it easy to speak to his step mum.

This helped to show him a) it was possible and b) it was potentially a good thing and something he could see a benefit in doing. It is making the whole thing more acceptable to the gatekeeper in his mind.

Obviously at this early stage, Carlos still held his old belief and his old belief was still the truth to him as he had no real evidence to the contrary.

To ensure the *new* belief had the best chance of taking root and growing, we needed to anchor it into his unconscious, through his conscious mind. Like any new skill/behaviour, the more you practice, the better you get. Changing a belief is exactly the same. So I asked Carlos what he did at least twelve times every day. He confirmed he checked his mobile phone or sent text messages regularly throughout the day, so this would become his anchor, the thing that would remind him to say his new belief, "I find it easy to talk to my step mum". He confirmed that he was totally committed to saying his new belief throughout the coming days and weeks, especially whenever he checked his phone or received a text.

Why do we use this anchoring technique? Whilst our subconscious mind still believes the old belief is true, we will conveniently forget to do the things we've promised to do. I'm sure you can think of a time when you've been trying to lose weight or exercise more, only to find yourself forgetting to buy the salad from the shop or double booking the time you'd set aside for your exercise class, because you we're basically proving your old beliefs right and returning to your old pattern of behaviour.

So anchoring just jogs our memory, reminding us we have committed to a new way of doing things, reminding us we have a new empowering belief to install. I am not suggesting that the affirmation of "I find it easy to talk to my step mum" is magically creating the change, but from my experience it keeps the awareness of the desired change in the forefront of your conscious mind and helps you to find the solutions you need to start supporting the new belief. This ensures you start to let the new evidence past the gatekeeper and thus giving the new empowering belief a quicker route to your subconscious mind.

Two weeks later, I rang the door bell and Carlos's step mum answered the door, "what have you done to Carlos?" she said smiling from ear to ear.

I laughed and asked what she meant. "Well, he's changed, he's much more talkative and sociable".

"Let me chat to Carlos and see what he's got to say about it" I replied.

I went through to the lounge where Carlos was sitting, we shook hands and Carlos smiled, one of those knowing smiles.

"So what's been going on?" I asked.

He replied, still smiling, "We went to the cinema, which was great. We've been out for a family meal and I've also spent more time sitting and chatting with the family at dinner time. My step mum has helped me with a few bits of course work and we've been getting along really well, it's been a really great couple of weeks"

"So what's changed?" I enquired.

"I guess I've just found it easier to talk to my step mum" he replied

He went on to say, not only had he been saying his new belief when he checked his phone, but he'd been saying it to himself when he cleaned his teeth in the morning and whenever he'd thought of it during the day, because it always made him laugh.

Carlos had successfully broken the pattern of his old *limiting* belief and replaced it with a more *empowering* belief, which meant he was starting to find evidence to support the new belief. This effectively allowed him to come up with new ways of doing things which would not have been possible had he maintained his old belief.

> *Change the way you look at things and the things you look at change.*

To me, beliefs are like pathways through the forrest of your subconscious mind, some of those pathways are very well trodden and those particular pathways seem to be the only way to get to where you're going. However, once you become aware some of your pathways are causing you problems and limiting where they can take you, I presume you'd be open to the suggestion of creating a new pathway through the forrest, wouldn't you? It may be a bit of challenge at first, because you're not used to walking this new path, however, the more often you use it, the more well trodden it becomes, until, before you know it, your old pathway is overgrown and your new pathway is the easiest way to get to where you want to go. In fact it'll be difficult for you to remember where the old pathway was, let alone why you ever used it in the first place.

You may think the grass is greener on the other side, but if you take the time to water your own grass it will be just as green.

Chapter

Pain and pleasure are the catalyst for change

Pain and pleasure are the catalyst for change

You can't force your child to change; you can only help them to change if they're ready and willing. As the saying goes "You can lead a horse to water, but you can't make it drink." Basically, they have got to have a good enough reason to *want* to change.

If I were a sports coach and my client wanted to lose weight and get a toned physique to run faster or jump higher, we would probably work on a certain diet and exercise programme which would get them fitter and toned, but if they didn't do the exercises we agreed upon and carried on eating an unhealthy diet, nothing would change. And as my good friend and mentor, Tony Robbins taught me long ago, people will only change their behaviour when either the end result (their goal) is pleasurable enough or the pain of their current situation is bad enough to make them consistently and permanently take the necessary actions to change their current pattern of behaviour.

As human beings we are basically driven to take action by moving towards pleasure or away from pain or a combination of the two. Think of it like this; Why do you go to work? Is it because you love it, therefore it's for the pleasure or is it because you have bills to pay and the thought of not being able to fulfil your commitments is not acceptable to you?

Bearing in mind the ultimate outcome of not paying your bills is to become homeless and I presume this really doesn't appeal to you? In which case you are moving away from the pain (shame or embarrassment) it would cause you to not honour your commitments (or to be homeless). You may well work to pay the bills, but actually you enjoy the social side of going to work and therefore one part of you is moving away from pain, while the other part of you is moving towards pleasure.

It is for this reason that I love working with youngsters who are being bullied. That sounds terrible I know, but it's true, because my job is made so much easier because their pain is so bad, they are willing to try anything to stop the bullying.

There are a number of if's and buts' when trying to help a youngster who's being bullied. First of all, they need to trust you enough to actually confide in you that there is a problem. By trust, I not only mean trust that you will listen, trust that you will give the situation the significance it deserves, but trust that you won't take the situation into your own hands and try and deal with things on their behalf, potentially making a bad situation a whole lot worse for them.

So *when you find yourself*.......

in the privileged position of a young person sharing with you, that they are being bullied, listen and listen some more. Listen to the words they use, because they are the words you'll need to use back to them to show them you understand, (not your interpretation of what they mean, but their actual words).

Find a quiet spot where they'll feel safe enough to continue and commit to being 100% present with them through this. If you haven't got time to do this now, then you need to put aside a time later that same day and go through it. Personally, I would drop everything to let a child talk to me about bullying, as it will have taken a lot for them to open up enough to ask for help and I'm conscious of taking those opportunities as soon as they are presented to me rather than putting them off. Our job, if we really want to help them get through this, is to help them come up with their *own* solutions, (not our suggested solutions). If you give your opinion or your solution to the problem, you are just another adult who doesn't really understand and although they'll say "I know, I know", they are very unlikely to actually take your advice, let alone act on it.

In my experience, when somebody says "I know" that really means, "I've just stopped listening".

Once they have shared with me that they're being bullied, I say something like, "so how many people are at your school?" they obviously reply with a

57

figure, let's say a thousand for the sake of this example.

I go on to ask "So does the bully, bully all one thousand students at your school?"

"No" is always the reply.

I continue with a friendly smile on my face, "so, what's so great about you, that they've chosen to bully you?" Now this last sentence may seem harsh, but it's designed to break the pattern of negative emotion and get them to start questioning things a little.

Can you see how that is better than using victim language like "Oh! You poor thing", which is not very helpful and only serves to make them feel sorry for themselves.

Now, the bully could be bullying them for all sorts of reasons, it could be that they've got a certain hair or skin colour, a big nose, they're too fat, too thin, too tall, too short, too rich, too poor, too clever, too stupid, the list is endless.

In my experience this just gets them ready for the next exercise which is the part, if done correctly, that will work *every* time and helps them to help themselves. It does this by changing *their* perception of the situation, *their* perception of the bully and *their* role in that particular relationship, because bullies will only bully people who will allow themselves to be bullied.

The best way I have found to help them come up with their own solution is an NLP (Neuro Linguistic Programming) technique called 'perceptual positioning' or the 'meta mirror'. A simple, but incredibly powerful technique for changing a person's perception or view of a situation or relationship. It involves disassociating from the experience so they can get a different perspective.

The steps

Position 1: Seeing the situation through their own eyes
Position 2: Seeing the situation through the eyes of the bully
Position 3: Looking at the situation as a third party
Position 4: Seeing the situation through their own eyes,
with new learning.

The process

Position 1. Help them to imagine standing in front of the person they are being bullied by as if they were really there. Ask them to be themselves and tell the bully exactly how they feel, ask them what they're thinking, confirm what they think the problem is. If they cry, let them cry, it's all good, but do not touch them if they are crying or try to console them, as you don't want to anchor that negative feeling. Just let them have their moment.

When they have said absolutely everything they want to say, get them to shake their arms and legs to enable them to shake off that particular state, then direct them to stand in position 2.

Position 2. Now stand them in the place they imagined the other person in (usually directly opposite position 1) and encourage them to stand the way the bully stands and act like the bully acts, use the voice of the bully and pretend to be the bully. This pretend version of the bully has just heard everything they said to them in position 1, so now it's the bullies chance to respond. Just encourage them to say whatever comes to mind, everything they think the bully would say.

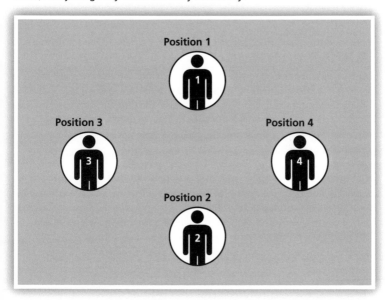

When they have said everything they want to say as the bully, encourage them to shake their arms and legs again to break their state and shake off "being the bully", then direct them from where they were standing and into position 3 (adjacent to position 1 and 2, like the points of a triangle.

Position 3. Now stand them in a position where they can 'see' the interaction that went on between themselves and the bully and encourage them to say what they are thinking and feeling as they look at the scene having heard what was said by both parties.

When they have answered the questions about what they are thinking and feeling, ask them to shake their arms and legs again to break state once again. Direct them into position 4. (next to position 1, as if they were whispering into their own ear, when they were in position 1.)

Position 4. In this position they can gain a view on all three positions as though they were not involved at all. They can pretend to be a fly on the wall or an expert in the field of bullying. Ask them what they would recommend or what advice would they give to themselves in position 1. When they have finished talking, encourage them to shake their arms and legs to break state once again.

Get them to go back to where they started in position 1 and ask how they feel now, how do they view the situation, ask them what's changed, what does the bully look like now.

The result

From experience the youngsters I go through this exercise with will come up with the best advice for themselves. It may be the same advice that you would have suggested, but by allowing them to come up with their own solution, they will follow through with it. They may still be fearful or apprehensive, but if done correctly, they will now have a different perception of the bully, the bully will be less significant, smaller, they may even feel sorry for them. They will have changed their role in the relationship with the bully, from that of a victim to that of someone more powerful. The bully will find it difficult to bully this individual anymore, because as I mentioned before, the bully will only pick on those individuals who allow themselves to be bullied. You will have helped the youngster change on the inside.

This is a simple, powerful and effective technique to assist that internal perceptual change. Like any new skill, it will take some practice to get it right. Get together with a group of other parents or teachers and practice with one another or better still, hire a local NLP practitioner to show you how to do it.

Alternatively you can log onto **www.darrencurtis.com** to find out when my next workshop is, where I can personally show you an example of how it works.

The sad thing is...

I think it's worth remembering that *any* type of bullying is actually a cry for help. If the bully is finding that many faults in others and are managing to make other's lives that miserable, just stop and think what *they* must be saying to themselves. Imagine what is going on or has gone on in the bullies life, that they are so afraid of letting go and asking someone for help. And believe me when I say they desperately need help, because they are the dog that barks and growls in the hall of a thousand mirrors. They've become so used to people growling and barking back, they think it's normal. The trick here is to break the pattern and wag your tail, do the opposite of what they expect, look for the good and when you find it (which you will), let them know you noticed it, they're just looking for someone to be proud of them too, they've just forgotten how easy it is to achieve.

Chapter

Praise their identity, discipline their behaviour

Praise their identity, discipline their behaviour

What you tell a child they are, is what they become. Tell a child they're stupid, irresponsible, a waste of space and that child will live down to your expectation.

Tell them they are amazing, they can be whatever they want to be, they're loved no matter what and they will live up to your expectation.

The voices of people who are significant to them, parents, teachers, guardians, siblings, close friends or carers become the voices in their heads when they have a decision to make.

When someone offers them a drug or cigarette for the first time, unconsciously they'll refer to their internal dialogue and ask "what would a stupid person do?", "What would a waste of space do?", "What would an irresponsible person do?", take the drug or cigarette, perhaps?

"What would an amazing person do?", "What would a person who is loved and secure do?", more than likely say, "no thanks, I'm ok".

When my son smashed the double glazed window at the back of our house, he came to me in tears and said "dad I'm really sorry, I broke the window". Now I could have said "*you* stupid idiot, how many times have I told you *not* to play football near the windows at the back of the house". Does this sound like something you're likely to say when you're angry or annoyed? Well, it's worth noting my points from chapter one, you've been telling them what you don't want, so it was inevitable to happen, take away the word "not" in the previous statement and I would have been planting the seeds for my son "to play football near the windows at the back of the house". Also, I would have been attacking his identity "*you* stupid idiot", is that really a belief about his identity I want him to carry around for the rest of his life? And I would have effectively been punishing him for coming to me and telling the truth. So what good would that do? Make him feel even worse, make him feel it's not good or safe to tell the truth?

What I actually said was "That was very honest of *you*, I really appreciate it when you're honest with me. I really appreciate *you* are such an honest person. Can you see why I tell you to play football at the *end* of the garden now?" If you're reading this, thinking, what a push over. I can assure you, I'm no push over and I'm all for the punishment to fit the crime, but let's be realistic here, what would I have been getting angry about? The cost of the replacement window, the time and hassle of replacing the window or the fact that he hadn't listened to me about playing at the rear of the garden (which some may perceive as being disrespectful). I went on to say, "so how are we going to pay for this?"

Bailey replied "well I guess I need to pay it out of my pocket money"

I have a very high value of fairness and it would have upset me to think of him paying the full price of replacing the window and I know I wouldn't have followed through on the punishment, which would send him the wrong message, but I did want to teach him a lesson. So I thanked him for his offer and said I felt it was fair if we paid half each, considering how honest he'd been.

We all make mistakes and sometimes we are punishing our children because they reflect back to us our own mistakes and how those mistakes make us feel or we overreact because they will have dishonoured one or more of our core values (e.g. respect, care, control, etc) or we simply have too much to do and they have just added to our stresses, but that's not *their* problem is it?

In this instance, Bailey was still punished for his mistake, but the cost was only £47.50, not his confidence, self esteem or a fear of being able to admit he'd made a mistake. Can you see how a few small changes in your reaction, will make a huge difference to your child's long term emotional well being?

A catch all statement is "I love you, but your behaviour is unacceptable"

When my kids leave for school in the morning I say "Enjoy yourselves, have a great day, learn lots, I love you."

When I was working at the University of California San Diego, I would go down the steep hill to the beach early in the morning to walk, relax and watch the surf dudes catching the early morning waves. On my way back to campus one morning, going back up the steep hill, I overtook a grand-mother with her grand-daughter trailing behind. I couldn't help over hearing their conversation;

"Nanny I'm tired, my legs are aching"

"You're lazy" replied the grand-mother as she picked up her grand-daughter.

I politely interrupted, hoping to help, "No, she's not lazy, she's got lots of energy"

I explained to the grand-mother the importance of identity, simply stating the power of how the "you're lazy" label she was giving her grand-daughter is probably not a good idea and the difference in outcome, if she were to give her grand-daughter a label of something more positive like "you're strong" or "you're a little bundle of energy".

The grand-daughters ears had been flapping all the time we'd been talking, when she suddenly jumps out of her grand-mothers arms and sprints the last 30 metres to prove to us how much energy she has, shouting "I'm strong and I'm a little bundle of energy". Her grand-mother asks why this sort of stuff isn't taught in schools? I don't have an answer to that question, but I'm sure it will be one day, when the decision makers catch up.

Children are sponges waiting to absorb life's experiences and learning's, which is why we have to be careful what we say to them and how we say it, as it is our words which shape their identity.

Remember, if you tell a child he/she is stupid and they will think they are stupid, stop trying and act stupid and your voice is the voice they'll hear inside their heads in their moments of decision in the months and years to come. Just like you and I, our children make thousands of decisions every

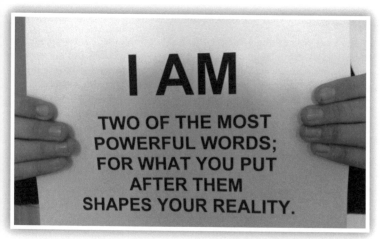

I AM

TWO OF THE MOST
POWERFUL WORDS;
FOR WHAT YOU PUT
AFTER THEM
SHAPES YOUR REALITY.

day, from the innocence of "should I use a red pen or blue pen?" to the more challenging, "should I say yes to this drug I'm being offered?" or "no, I'm fine thanks". If you're child isn't behaving how you would like them to, then think back to some of the phrases you've used to describe them, are they positive or negative? Good or bad? I will go into this in more depth throughout the book, but I like stories, so if you're sitting comfortably, I shall begin...

I was chatting with a teacher who shared with me that a lot of her students aren't very good with written English, especially story writing. One of her colleagues gets so frustrated he persists in telling them all how bad they are! Believe me when I say, they already tell themselves "I'm crap at English" or "I find this difficult". To add insult to injury, their English teacher is confirming to them, yes, you're right, you're terrible at English, in fact "You're so bad, I don't know why I even bother to turn up." Of course you can tell them where or how they could improve to help them move forward, but please imagine your voice in their heads and how it will sound? "You're a waste of space, you may as well give up" which translates in their head to "I'm a waste of space, I may as well give up" or "You've got the brains of a rocking horse" translates to "I've got the brains of a rocking horse".

The flip side to this is something more positive like "The more you focus, the better you'll get", even if you're exasperated by their lack of progress, you are installing a new belief that says "The more I focus the better I'll get" and that my friend is the first step to changing how they speak to themselves and because we human beings always want to prove ourselves right, they will start to find ways to get better using the latter statement.

A good example of this is the fact that I didn't finish reading a whole book until I was about thirty years old. I had started many books, but never actually finished any. I'd fall asleep any time I tried to read or I'd lose my place and read the same sentences over and over again, so I eventually gave up. Until that was, when I started to learn the powerful effects of how we talk to ourselves and how what you say on the inside has a direct impact on what you experience on the outside.

> *What you say on the inside has a direct impact on what you experience on the outside.*
>
> **Darren Curtis - (Author)**

I went from saying "I hate reading books" or "Reading makes me go to sleep" or "I've never finished a book", which at the time was all true, to saying "I love reading books" which was definitely not true back then. I would stand in front of the mirror in the morning brushing my teeth, smiling and repeating my new mantra "I love reading books". I would laugh to myself, knowing that this was complete and utter bull, but I persisted in my experiment and before long, I found that I seemed to have a book with me wherever I went. I signed up to an evening class, where I'd have to do a lot of reading about photography and another where I'd have to read extensively about hypnotic language patterns. Since then I've read many books on subjects which fascinate me and I genuinely do now love to read books.

The more positive an identity you can create, the easier your life will be and the easiest way to think of this is every time you say "you" or "you're" when addressing a child, you are potentially adding to that child's identity. So as I outlined earlier, your "you's" become their "I's" (ie. "you're an idiot", becomes "I'm an idiot" in their head).

> *In the moments of decision they will unconsciously hear your voice in their heads.*
>
> **Darren Curtis (Author)**

So it amazes me when I work in schools and I hear a teacher in the next room verbally destroying a youngster with statements like "You're a waste of space" or "You stupid little child".

What possible outcome are they looking for when these negative statements are launched at their students; surely they didn't get into teaching because they hated children and wanted to destroy their self esteem? This is not to say that you can't get annoyed or tell a child off, of course you can, but you must direct your frustrations and annoyance at their behaviour, not their identity.

If you insist on using negative language, I would suggest you change "you're an idiot" to "You're acting like an idiot" and change "You're irresponsible" to "I will not tolerate your irresponsible behaviour" etc. So you're able to let the child know there's a problem and you're not happy, but you are no longer attacking them as an individual.

What would be even better is to focus on what you want by saying "I want you to be more responsible" or "Please be sensible and behave", so you're now getting the child to focus on responsibility, being sensible and behaving.

These simple tweaks to your communications will have the effect of avoiding a whole lot of trouble in the future.

I was speaking to a nurse who shared a story about her son, she told me how he used to get all the pots and pans out in the kitchen when he was little and he would stand on a stool to mix all sorts of things together to make them fizz and bubble. She went on to tell me how she used to rub his hair and say "how's my little professor getting on today?".

Today that young child has become one of the youngest people to become a professor in England. I don't know about you, but I don't know too many professors and this chap has not only managed to achieve it, but achieved it in less time than normal and I have no doubt this was assisted by having a mum who gave him the label of "my little professor" instead of "you messy little git".

" *Kids become what you tell them they are.* "

Darren Curtis (Author)

So ask yourself this question, What identities do I give those around me?

If you're a parent, what identity are you giving to your child or children?

If you're a teacher what phrases do you use with your most challenging students?

If it's positive, thank you and well done, you're a great parent/teacher. If it's negative, I know you haven't been doing it deliberately, like many parents you've probably never realised the affects of attacking a child's identity. But now you do know and with this knowledge comes responsibility and I urge you to take the first step and turn those negative "you's" into positive "you's" and see how much easier your life gets when the "challenging" kids start to become what you tell them you'd like them to be.

Take a moment now, to write down some of the negative phrases you may have used in the past. The more honest you are with yourself now, the more effective this exercise will be.

Negative phrases I have used include ...

Positive phrases I could replace them with might be something like ...

_____

_____

_____

_____

_____

_____

_____

_____

_____

Chapter

Winning the game

Winning the game

An interesting trend I've found in infant and junior schools over the past two decades is to have non competitive sports days. A contradiction in terms, as by its very nature, sports are supposed to be competitive – are they not?

The educational decision makers claim that taking part in traditional races can be difficult and often embarrassing for many less physically able children.

Never mind the fact, often this is the only area the more physically able youngsters can excel and therefore know what it feels like to be one of the best for a day. To feel like a winner, to show off their physical intelligence and gain the respect of their peers, to be significant.

> *Always remember the importance of helping a child to feel significant.*
>
> **Darren Curtis - Author**

My take on this is, many of the decision makers in education may not have been very good at sport themselves and remember how crap it felt on sports day to be one of the last children to cross the winning line. No matter how hard they tried, they were never going to be recognised with a 2nd or 3rd place medal or rosette, let alone winning. In the main, this would have been a very unfamiliar place for them, as the education system suited their way of learning, having been designed by people who learn the same way. They would excel academically and go on to create more examinations and measurements to suite children who learn like they did, so the next generation like them can excel and feel good about themselves, maybe?

How interesting then, the children who are not academic are constantly measured against criteria which make them feel like a loser every single day. It is made blatantly clear who the clever kids are (measured on the current academic standards) and it is the clever kids who are given recognition and positive re-enforcement for their achievements, not just by being graded as achieving a*, a and b grades, but by the very fact of having top, middle and bottom sets.

What point are you trying to make? You may well ask.

I remember watching a child at a junior school sports day, who was getting very frustrated during an egg and spoon race because she was a bit slower than the rest of her classmates to begin with and found it even harder to run and balance the egg on the spoon at the same time. No matter how hard she tried, she kept dropping the egg and got further and further behind until she got so frustrated, she threw her egg and spoon on the ground, close to tears, she stormed off the track without finishing. A teacher tried to console her, telling her not to worry, it's ok, not everyone can be good at sport and the fact that it just wasn't her thing. The teacher then went on to comfort her further by reminding her how good she was at other things in the class room. Obviously, I commend the teacher for noticing a child is struggling, for taking the time to make them feel good about themselves and helping to change her perspective on the situation. It's also worth noting that those words, spoken by that teacher on that day, will be adding to that child's positive, encouraging internal voice in her years to come. Remember it is our voice, the words we chose to speak to them as children, that becomes the future internal voice as they grow from a youngster to a teenager and into an adult.

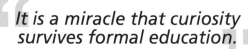

It is a miracle that curiosity survives formal education.

Albert Einstein

My observation that day, led me to this question, when a below average student (measured academically) just doesn't understand what the teacher is trying to teach in the class room. No matter how hard they try, they find themselves falling further and further behind, until they eventually get so frustrated, they explode with emotion and often leave the classroom without finishing. Does that same teacher show the same respect and understanding, telling them not to worry, it's ok, not everyone can be good at (insert chosen subject) and the fact that it just isn't their thing and remind them that they're really good at something else? or does that same teacher, let the youngster know in no uncertain terms that their behaviour is not acceptable, they are at best punished with detention or worse made to stand alone with no support to stew over how stupid they feel, with their internal voice screaming "everybody else gets it, why can't I", "I'm thick, I'm stupid, I'm dumb", "There's no hope for me", "I hate that bloody teacher", "I hate School", "What's the bloody point" etc, etc

What's the difference between these two scenarios? We currently live in a society, where our children's lives are measured against somebody else's values and criteria of success. How different would it be if children were measured on how confident they are, how healthy they are, how much emotional intelligence they had, how persuasive they were, how effectively they managed money, how easily they found it to create and maintain relationships?

The key skills necessary for a long, happy and fulfilling work and personal life.

> *The original Olympian ideal is held by recognising truth, strength and beauty as well as speed or distance, in this way the qualities of each child are honoured.*

Greek Olympian

The theory of multiple intelligences was developed in 1983 by Dr. Howard Gardner, professor of education at Harvard University. It suggests the traditional notion of intelligences, based on I.Q. testing, is far too limited. Dr. Gardner proposes eight different intelligences to account for a broader range of human potential in children and adults. These intelligences are;

Linguistic Intelligence ("word smart")
Logical-mathematical Intelligence ("number/reasoning smart")
Spatial Intelligence ("picture smart")
Bodily-Kinesthetic Intelligence ("body smart")
Musical Intelligence ("music smart")
Interpersonal intelligence ("people smart")
Intrapersonal Intelligence ("self smart")
Naturalist Intelligence ("nature smart")

Dr. Gartner says that our schools and culture focus most of their attention on linguistic and logical-mathematical intelligence. We esteem the highly articulate or logical people of our culture. However, Dr. Gartner says that we should also place equal attention on individuals who show gifts in the other intelligences: the artists, architects, musicians, naturalists, designers, dancers, therapists, entrepreneurs, and others who enrich the world in which we live. Unfortunately, many children who have these gifts don't receive much reinforcement for them in school. Many of these kids, in fact, end up being labelled "learning disabled", "ADD (Attention Deficit Disorder)", or simple under achievers, when their unique ways of thinking and learning aren't addressed by a heavily linguistic or logical-mathematical classroom.

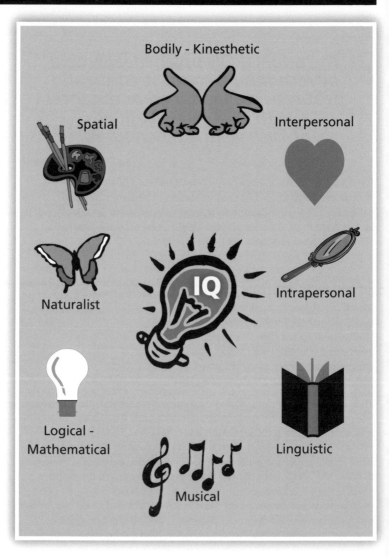

The theory of multiple intelligences proposes a major transformation in the way our schools are run. It suggests that teachers be trained to present their lessons in a wide variety of ways using music, cooperative learning, art activities, role play, multimedia, field trips, inner reflection, and much more. The good news is that the theory of multiple intelligences has grabbed the attention of many educators around the world, and hundreds of schools are currently using its philosophy to redesign the way it educates children. The bad news is that there are thousands of schools still out there that teach in the same old dull way, through dry lectures, and boring worksheets and textbooks. The challenge is to get the information out to many more teachers, school administrators, and others who work with children, so that each child has the opportunity to learn in ways harmonious with their unique minds.

Our job as parents and teachers is to recognise what each child is good at and nurture it, to make them feel better about themselves by acknowledging their strengths rather than highlighting their weaknesses.

Rob Parsons puts it so well in his book "TEENAGERS – what every parent has to know".

"Imagine the scene: our teenage daughter comes home with her school report. She's got an A in History, a B in Maths and a D in French. What do we spend most of the next hour talking about? The French of course? We say, "How can we help you do better in your French? Shall we get you some study guides in GCSE French? How about some audio tapes or perhaps a tutor?

Where's the parent who will say, 'Let's get you a tutor for your History!"

"But, Mum, I got an A in History!"

"I know. Let's make you even better at what you're already good at."

I understand the need to get a spread of GCSE's – and the pressure therefore of trying to keep all the plates in the air – but especially with the seemingly less able child, it's vital to send them into life knowing that they have found at least one strength and that they have a parent who is helping them to develop it."

> *Let them know you love them irrespective of their achievements.*[1]

Rob Parsons – Author

What is your child really good at?

Where do they have natural talent?

What can you do to encourage their natural talent?

Chapter

Pick your battles

Pick your battles

When you transfer your frustration and anger from one battle to the next, to the next, you are literally fighting a series of losing battles. In the past you may have found yourself stacking your emotions, building up a barrier of resentment and unfortunately resentment only leads to blame and blame doesn't help you or your child. And whilst you're busy blaming others it blinds you to the many options you have available to you.

The common battles I come across are, the untidy room battle, the doing your homework at the last minute battle, the coming home late battle, the spending too much time on the games console battle, the talking with your mouth full battle, the not pulling your weight around house battle, insert your favourite battle here battle!! The list goes on.

The problem is you are probably moaning as much about the trivial things as you are about the more serious things, so the punishment or severity of the moaning doesn't necessarily fit the crime and this will often come across as being unfair (remember the values chapter, especially if you have a child with a high value of fairness, their reaction to any feeling of injustice or unfairness will be extreme). The more battles you are trying to win the more stacked emotion you will have stored and therefore the more challenging you may find it to let go, especially if *you* have a high value of control.

When you break down how much time you spend moaning, nagging or being stressed, I would estimate eighty percent of your emotional strength is used up on just one ongoing battle and the remaining twenty percent is used up on the rest. So it makes sense to put your energy into fixing the one battle which is causing you the most grief.

If you could only win one battle, what's the most important battle for you to win?

Remember the story from the first chapter, where the mum was getting annoyed about so many different things, but when she chose to focus her efforts on the main battle she would like to win, the battle that caused eighty percent of the arguments in her home, I was able to help her to find a solution. You're sharing your life with other human beings, some of whom are going through lots of emotional and physical changes and if you can learn to focus on the thing that will give you the greatest result for the least amount of effort, I would suggest you go for solving that one thing. After all, it can be tiring for you and them if you are constantly trying to get everyone to do everything *you* want and who says what *you* want is the right thing anyway?

Live through deeds of love, and let others live with tolerance for their unique intentions.

Rudolf Steiner

The following may help with your perception behind some of the battles;

With every action or communication we have an intention, the person or people at the receiving end of our action or communication will interpret what it means, depending on the interpretation they give it, there will be a resulting impact.

I call this the three 'i' triangle.

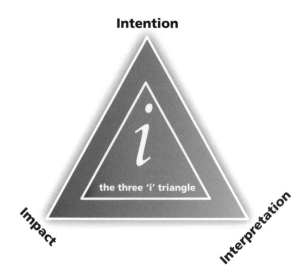

Intention

the three 'i' triangle

Impact

Interpretation

Let's imagine you ask your child to tidy their room, your intention is to get some order so you can feel relaxed, their interpretation is you're nagging, your child doesn't clean their room, their intention is to relax, your interpretation is they're being disrespectful, therefore the impact is that you get annoyed and shout at them, they shout back, you have a argument.

Which is interesting because both of your intentions were the same, but everyone misinterpreted what the other meant.

You ask if they have any homework, your intention is to be helpful. Their interpretation is you're nagging, the impact is they grunt at you. Their intention at this point is to be left alone, you interpret this as rude, the impact is this annoys you, you have an argument.

If you could have held on to your original intention of being helpful and understand how they had misinterpreted what you meant, you could have continued trying to be helpful or maybe the biggest help could have been to have left them alone, which is what they wanted, and let them face the consequence of not doing their homework. Learning the lesson of consequence will help their roots to grow, it challenges them to be more independent, to not have to rely on you so much (unless of course, it's part of your agenda for them to rely on you, because you like to feel needed, even though you moan about it?) Can you see the paradox's we get ourselves into from time to time?

I remember chatting to a colleague who felt her son was spending too much time on his games console in his bedroom. She was really concerned that at Sixteen years old he was spending hours on end in his room with his mates and their world seemed to revolve around *those* senseless games, (her words not mine), but does this sound familiar? When I asked what her main concern was, she said she felt he should be spending more time playing outside and less time wasting his life in his bedroom.

I remember sharing with her a story about a parent whose main battle was getting her Fifteen year old son to come home at night. He would often stay out into the early hours of the morning, getting drunk or smoking green leafy substances.

My colleague looked at me in sheer horror saying "oh! my god, I'm so lucky to know where my son is every night, he's such a good lad, he does really well at school and he has a really good group of friends. Him spending time in his room seems quite insignificant now doesn't it? I'm going to go home and give him a hug and tell him how much I appreciate him."

We all do it don't we? We get so wrapped up in what seems like a battle, but actually it's completely trivial in the grand scheme of things. It's often something we have blown up out of all proportion, because we sometimes need something or someone to put our situation with our own children back into perspective to allow us to appreciate all the good things about them and our own ability to parent.

> *When I was a boy and I wanted to learn to swim, I tried my hardest to thrash about in the water, but the harder I tried, the quicker I sank? I thought to myself, what would happen if I tried to do the opposite? So I completely relaxed, I trusted and I just let go, hey-presto! I could float. This is something I keep reminding myself in life, when I remember to relax, trust and let go, I float.*

Darren Curtis - (Author)

What three areas would you be willing to relax, trust and let go of?

1...

2...

3...

Chapter

eleven

Listening

Listening

I'm sure you'll agree, the greatest gift you can give to anyone is the gift of attention and the best form of attention is to listen. When a child wants to talk, listen. It may not always be the most interesting of conversations, but they have chosen to chat to you about what is important to them at that moment in time and by paying them the courtesy of stopping what you are doing and listening, you are sending them a very clear message; "You're important to me", "You are significant". Kids who grow up feeling important and significant don't need to seek it elsewhere later in life by joining gangs or taking drugs, especially during the teenage years.

When I've asked teenagers what they want from their parents, they will reply;

"I want my parents to feel I'm someone special". Let them know they are special to you. Remember Craig and what he was willing to do to make his mum proud?

"I want my parents to be warm and friendly to me, just like when they answer the door or the phone". Isn't it funny how we often keep our most focused listening for strangers and treat the people we love with the most disregard?

> ❝ *My dad's always telling me what he does for me, I wish my dad would do less for me and more with me.* ❞
>
> a 13 year old boy

Consider this, a child who is used to being told to shut up or told to come back later because you're too busy (a slightly more polite way of saying shut up) will eventually stop trying to communicate. So don't be surprised when they become a teenager who just grunts at you most of the time, exercising their new found freedom to do as they wish and somewhere in the back of their head, their interval voice will be saying "they never listen to me, so why bother talking to them". We all have a need to be listened to and if they don't feel listened to by you, who are they finding to listen to them? Because this person now has a significant influence over your child. If you invest in listening early on, you will reap the rewards as they grow, as it will be you they turn to for advice and guidance instead of the person you have no control over.

There are three kinds of listening, there is the conversational style of listening, often referred to as the "*me too*" method of listening. This is what we all commonly use for day to day interactions with people. Generally they say something and while they are talking you are listening, but you are also relating the subject to something in your life, so you can answer when they stop talking. The amount of information you actually hear will depend on how interested you were in the person or subject.

The second kind of listening is *active* listening. This is where your mind is empty, you have no pre-conceived ideas or judgement, you are really listening to what the person is saying, allowing them the time and space to express themselves. Your only interest is on them, you are not interested in yourself. This type of listening takes some practice, but it is an extremely useful way to build strong relationships, especially with your partner and children.

Thirdly, there is dynamic listening, where you are listening to what's not being said, you can hear what's going on behind a conversation. Once again, this is listening in it's purest form and this is usually only for what I call professional listeners who are good at their jobs (i.e. some psychologists, counsellors and coaches). The reason I say "some", like in any profession you get people who are good at what they do and others who aren't so good.

So often I hear parents and teachers telling children they need to *learn to listen*, but where exactly should they learn this skill from. It's certainly not taught in schools and the majority of teachers I know find it extremely hard to listen because their job is primarily to speak, share information, to *teach* (not listen).

Listening is a skill that takes some practice and I would suggest we all need to learn to listen more. A great way to teach a child to listen is to sit down with them one to one and ask some open questions and listen to their reply.

Try asking these questions;

What's your favourite thing to do?

What is it about that particular thing that you enjoy?

What's your favourite memory?

What is it about that particular memory that you like?

What do you wish we could do more of?

If they ever say, "I don't know", say "if you did know the answer, what would it be?"

If they really don't know, just leave it and go on to the next question. It's just a bit of fun.

Give them time to answer. If they don't answer immediately, allow them a bit of silence to think if necessary. Silence is a good thing, it means they're considering their reply.

Remember, the purpose of the exercise is for you to really listen, no pre-conceived ideas, no judgement, no right or wrong, no adding in what you think. You are giving them the time and space to express themselves and by doing so you will find out a bit more about your child. You may be surprised what you learn, when you just shut up and listen.

You will also be leading by example, teaching your child how to listen and demonstrating that you care enough to ask questions *and* listen to the answers.

Proper listening will also help to avoid a whole lot of arguments, as often it's the absence of proper listening which causes the misunderstanding or misinterpretation in the first place, (refer back to the three 'i' triangle in chapter 9). If you spend ten extra seconds listening, you may save yourself ten minutes of arguing and possibly ten years of regret about words you didn't mean to say, all because you bothered to listen.

Some personality types are much more emotional in their responses than others, but I'm sure you'll agree that teenagers love to respond with emotional. This is ok, it's normal.

Think of all your best memories from childhood, they will all have emotions attached to them, parties, Christmas, holidays, etc. Creating an environment which is conducive to talking makes such a difference, which is why eating together as a family is so important. I personally take each of my boys away every year, just me and one of them for at least a long weekend to chat, share stories and chill out. It allows us to spend uninterrupted time together on a one to one basis, whilst the other one stays at home with his mum and they too get some quality one to one time together.

Encourage them to get out and about, to do things with you from an early age so it becomes a habit and you'll reap the benefits as you grow together. If they have an interest, show an interest, even if it's not strictly your thing.

Your relationship with your children is like an emotional bank account that you are either adding to or taking away from. If you don't ensure that your emotional bank account stays in credit, the costs can start to add up in the form of their performance at school, poor behaviour, poor choice of friends, desire to spend less and less time with you, the list is endless. When it comes to your kids the amount of time and effort you put in with them today will pay dividends as they get older. If you listen to them, they will return the favour later on by listening to you, listening to your advice, listening to your requests. You will have taught them *by example*. If you take the time to sit down and talk, you will have established a communications channel they have been used to using and one they trust works. If you want to kid yourself that you are too busy and have to regularly work late, you're sending them a clear signal "my work is more important than you", which seems to have a habit of turning around and biting you on the arse later on. Sure you'll have a great bank account and feel significant at work, but you'll feel like shit when you wake up one morning and realise you haven't got a relationship with your son or daughter.

When do you intend to sit down and give them a good listening to?

Date:

> **❝** *If you don't listen eagerly to the little stuff when they are little, they won't tell you the big stuff when they are big, because to them all of it has always been big stuff.* **❞**
>
> Catherine M. Wallace

Chapter

Perception is reality

Perception is reality

Picture the scene, a pair of 1930's semi-detached homes, blackened broken windows and charred window frames, most of the roof missing, except for some charcoal smouldering woodwork which used to hold the roof and roof tiles in position, both homes completely destroyed by fire. The fire engines are still spraying water onto the roof to ensure no secondary fires start, but it is clear that absolutely everything inside both homes is burnt to a cinder. A man is sitting on the curb outside the house on the left with his head in his hands, his wife and children although clearly distressed, are trying to comfort him. He looks extremely angry and you overhear him commenting to his wife and children, "this is the last bloody straw, why does this crap always happen to us? As if life isn't bad enough already, what have I done to deserve this? We've lost everything, I must be the unluckiest man in the world".

You turn to see a car pull up outside the house on the right, a man jumps out and runs to his wife and children who are standing by the fire engine, with the biggest smile on his face, he throws his arms around them and declares "thank god, you're all ok, it's only stuff, we can replace all the stuff, I love you all so much, I am truly the luckiest man in the world". The event is the same for both parents, but their perceptions are worlds apart. Can you see the way they have viewed the situation speaks volumes about what they demonstrate to others as being important to them.

Ever notice how, when something happens in a teenagers life, they exaggerate the story and blow it up to be something much more than it really is? Does this annoy you? Which one of your values does this dishonour? Maybe honesty? but if you know that most teenagers are going to exaggerate, why not just let them, but view it from a different angle, change your perception. Maybe their intention is to make the story more interesting? Maybe their intention is to be more significant in the story or to you? If you can change your perception of your teenager's behaviour, then a positive change in your reaction to your teenager's behaviour will automatically follow.

The power of a positively framed question

Your brain loves to answer the questions you pose to yourself. If you pose a negative question your brain will usually reply with an equally negative answer and it's worth re-emphasising once again that you will be trying to prove yourself right e.g.

Negative question "Why do they *always* answer me back?"

Possible negative answer "Because they don't respect me"

Negative question "Why won't they do as they're told?"

Possible negative answer "Because they're trying to annoy me"

It is much better to ask yourself a positively framed question to allow your brain to work on a positive solution.

Positive question "What can I do to *gain* more respect?"

Possible positive answer "Be consistent, have more self respect and ask for what I want"

Positive question "What needs to happen to encourage them to listen to me?"

Possible positive answer "stay calm and lead by example"

If you feel that life has gotten a bit too serious, allow yourself to lighten up and laugh a little more.

The magic of Metaphor

If you hear yourself saying things like "being a parent is an uphill struggle" or "I seem to be taking two steps forwards and one step back", your brain not only builds a vivid picture of the problem, it now has emotion linked to it and it says to itself, "Here's a statement, it's a fact, lets go and find some more evidence to prove ourselves right" (refer to chapter one and chapter 6).

It is much more useful to eliminate any negative metaphors and replace them with brighter, more positive images for the brain to work on. It is better for you to choose your own so it is something personal and unique to you, but to give you an idea, something like "being a parent is a wonderful journey" or "I seem to be progressing in leaps and bounds" would be the positive alternatives to the previous negative metaphors. So your brain now says, "ok we've got *new* statements and images to work with, lets go and find some new evidence to prove ourselves right"

You may be saying to yourself at this point, no Darren, my brain is saying "that's a lie, I don't believe being a parent is a wonderful journey and I don't seem to be progressing in leaps and bounds" and I respect that, but we want to loosen the grip of the old metaphors which are no longer serving you or your family and I'm presuming by reading this far you're open to trying something a little different to help you to get a favourable end result? (remember the fly at the window?)

This exercise will help.

Answer the following question, coming up with at least four options for each question.

What can I do to help make my life as a parent a wonderful journey?

1. _____

_____

2. _____

_____

3. _____

_____

4. _____

_____

What can I do to help myself progress in leaps and bounds?

1. _____

_____

2. _____

_____

3. _____

_____

4. _____

_____

_____

Draw a picture of your new metaphor (just a basic picture is fine, relax and let go, use colour, the more child like the better).

Past examples from parents have been;

"life is like a bowl of cherries"

"Communicating with my children is as easy as shelling peas"

And finally go and buy yourself a postcard, fridge magnet or picture which represents your new metaphor.

People often ask me if I'm aiming for some type of utopia for families. This makes me smile, because I love the confidence which often comes out of adversity and some of the most interesting people I know would not have the strength of character they have today without the challenges they were presented with in their formative years.

However, the years leading up to being a teenager and throughout the teenage years are important as a right of passage for our children. They are learning lots of life's lessons and are in unfamiliar territory, often resulting in conflict in the home or school. So my main aim is actually for our children to grow into happy, healthy, confident adults, able to make good choices, cope with the challenges life will throw their way and for them to fulfil their potential. After all it is the trees which grow in stormy, windy climates, where the weather challenges then to grow stronger, thicker, deeper roots which enable them to stay upright.

> *What happens to a man is less significant than what happens within him.*
>
> Louis L. Mann

When you allow yourself to view a child from a completely different perspective, you will also be allowing your relationship to change for the better.

Remember I've been sharing with you, how we consistently try and prove ourselves right depending on the beliefs we hold about a certain person, situation or yourself. If you believe little Johnny is an attention seeking pain in the arse, you'll find every shred of evidence to support your negative belief.

If you can find it in yourself to believe that little Johnny is trying his best and appreciate Johnny has other qualities which you are committed to uncovering, you will find you're calmer and more forgiving of the things that used to wind you up about little Johnny.

This is why you have to be so careful if you have favourites. Favouritism can be just as damaging for the child who's the favourite as well as the child who's not.

The Harry Potter films beautifully illustrate to us the downside of favouritism, as we all root for Harry against his very spoilt cousin Dudley Dursley. You can see how Harry can never get anything right in his Aunt and Uncles eyes and Dudley can never get anything wrong. Harry does everything to try to please them in the beginning, but as they always find

99

fault, so eventually Harry gives up trying. On the other hand Dudley is not allowed to grow as an individual because his mother and father are constantly doing everything for him.

Let them know, they are loved unconditionally, they are safe and they belong, but also challenge them often to do things outside of their comfort zone. This will build resilience, independence and significance, to slowly and safely improve their confidence.

We *all* crave significance in some way and if a child can't find a way to achieve this in a positive way, they will achieve it in a negative way.

A child that hits another child, is significant to the other child in that moment.

A teenager who smokes a cigarette or takes a drug wants to show off, act older or belong – showing off, acting older and a desire to belong are all a need for significance.

A youngster who becomes the leader of a gang, has gained the significance they crave. The teenager who carries a knife or a gun gains a forced respect/fear from their peers and therefore also has their need for significance met.

You'd think that throwing a child in at the deep end would toughen them up, wouldn't you? And calling them a wimp because they can't or won't do it, will definitely make them more confident, won't it?

No, no, no, of course not, it is more likely to have the totally opposite effect to building confidence and significance and is more likely to lead to anxiety, uncertainty, self doubt and can make them feel like a failure.

Simple things like encouraging your child to take items back to the shop when they're younger and allowing them to ask the shop assistant or cashier if they can exchange things or ordering their own food in a cafe or restaurant, instead of relying on you to do it for them, will help them to become a better and more confident communicator and to feel more significant in a positive way.

"Encourage and support are the key"

What things would you like to change right now?

What would you like to start doing?

What would you like to stop doing?

" *Give your child the roots to grow and the wings to fly.*"

Jim Rohn

Chapter

Eat, drink and be happy...

Eat, drink and be happy...

Some parents hire me to work with their children who have been diagnosed with Attention Deficit Hyperactivity Disorder (ADHD), anger management or behavioural issues. I'll start by asking who diagnosed the condition? The reply is usually a doctor. My next question is "what did they say about diet?"

"Nothing" is usually the reply.

How can any responsible medical professional prescribe drugs with serious side effects to a child without finding out what they consume to begin with?

Starting where I believe the doctors should have started, I ask the youngster to write down every thing they've eaten and drank in the last twenty four hours. The following is a list I got from a recent client;

7:00am	Cereal and milk (one of the main ingredients of the cereal was sugar)
8:00am	Chocolate bar and can of coke on the way to school (main ingredients of sugar and caffeine)
10:20am	Energy drink (main ingredients of sugar and caffeine)
1:00pm	Hot dog, chips and energy drink (High fat, high sugar)
3:20pm	Crisps and can of coke on the way home from school (high fat, high sugar, caffeine)
3:45pm	Biscuits and crisps (high fat, high sugar)
5:00pm	Cheese and tomato pizza and chips and can of coke (high fat, high sugar, high caffeine)
6:30pm	Energy drink (high sugar and high caffeine)
8:00pm	Cereal and milk (high sugar)

If one of my boys had half the aforementioned diet for just one day, I wouldn't want to be in the same room as him. He'd be rude, restless, obnoxious, annoying, answering me back, the list of negative behaviour would be endless, we would definitely argue and the sad thing is, it wouldn't actually be *his* fault, I'd be arguing with a dehydrated, sugar and caffeine fuelled lunatic.

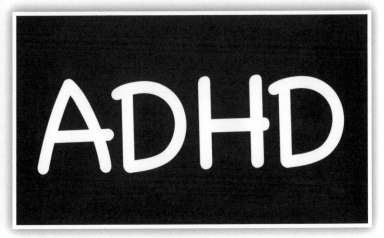

This child has not got ADHD. They are consuming too much sugar, too much caffeine, too much processed food and not enough still water, fruit and vegetables.

If you go back to basics, healthy food and drink will help you and your child to be calmer and happier. What they eat is a habit and it is up to you to help them change any unhealthy eating habits. I'm conscious that it is likely any unhealthy eating habits are usually inherited, so if you're serious about helping your child to have better moods and behaviour, may I be so bold as to suggest you take ownership of what you eat as a family. If *you* are not eating enough healthy food (e.g. fruit, vegetables, non-processed foods) and drinking enough still water, then *you* need to make the necessary changes to start introducing these foods.

The water content of the average healthy person is 60% water, interestingly in someone who is obese this reduces to Forty Five percent. It's worth noting we often get confused between the signal from the brain to let us know we are thirsty, interpreting this signal as hunger, so we are effectively eating when we should be drinking water. The rule of thumb here is to have a glass of water each time you feel hungry, then wait for ten minutes, If you still feel hungry, eat.

The majority of our brain is comprised of water and when fully hydrated we have clarity of thought, we find it easier to concentrate and it has a positive effect on our mood. In fact, dehydration is a significant cause of headaches and when you and I have a headache I'm sure you'll agree we are a lot less tolerant of any negative behaviour. Is that because our children's behaviour got worse? No, our level of tolerance dropped, but the good news is you can control the number of headaches you get and therefore improve your tolerance levels by making some minor tweaks to your diet and by being conscious of the type and amount of fluid you and/or your child consumes.

A really simple way to know that you and your child is getting a minimal quota of water is to buy or fill a 1.5 litre bottle of water and take regular

sips throughout the day with the aim of consuming all the water by the end of the day. In my experience this one simple tweak to your routines will amount to a significant improvement in yours and your teenagers general mood and tolerance levels.

It is so important to consume the fruits and vegetables which contain the trace minerals, the vitamins and anti-oxidants we so vitally need to maintain our health and help to regulate our moods even further. By adding these things into yours and your child's diet you will find you are calmer and more able to cope with the day to day challenges which occur, especially where teenagers are involved.

After visiting a nutritionist I found I was lacking in zinc and magnesium. After seeking out foods which were higher in these minerals and taking a good quality "true food" mineral supplement everyday, I found my mood improved significantly. If I'm easily stressed or agitated these days my kids actually joke "have you taken your minerals today dad". So it's worth getting yours or your child's mineral levels checked by a professional nutritionist prior to going down the drugs route.

What have I eaten and drank in the last 24 hours.

What has my child eaten and drank in the last 24 hours.

Chapter

fourteen

Keep calm and carry on...

Keep calm and carry on...

I'm always interested in how you know you're having a good day or a bad day. What emotions are you experiencing which let you know you're having a good day? Happiness, calm, excitement, joy, peace, harmony, choose or add the words which resonate with you.

On a bad day you may be feeling anger, annoyance, irritation, upset, guilt, depression, jealousy, fear, confusion, again choose or add the words which resonate with you.

All of the aforementioned positive emotions put us in a resourceful state, where we can connect with our children and get the best from them. The negative emotions create an un-resourceful state where we are likely to say things we regret, attack, blame and bring out the worst in our children.

Although it can be common to have a completely good day or a completely bad day, I'm sure you'll agree, you and I will generally experience a range of emotions throughout a given day or week.

We can be going along merrily, feeling positive emotions, then suddenly someone or something happens which makes us flip to the negative emotions and I like to refer to these as *triggers*. If somebody says something to annoy you, how you interpreted what they said was the trigger. If you suddenly feel overwhelmed, the last thing you took on was the trigger. We all have different triggers depending on our values and beliefs, so something which will be annoying to you may well slip past somebody else without being noticed. (remember the story of the youngsters in the alleyway and the perceived disrespect in chapter 4?)

Similarly, if your child does something to make you feel proud and you've taken the time to notice, it can easily take you from feeling a negative emotion to a positive emotion of sheer joy in an instance. Something as simple as someone showing you some appreciation, may help you go from being annoyed to feeling really happy or dare I say *appreciated*. But once again, the trick is to notice when you're being appreciated and this may involve changing any negative beliefs you may hold regarding how appreciated you currently feel.

But we don't have to be dependent on others to change our emotions, the most important thing to realise is that we all have our own triggers for helping us to go from a un-resourceful state to a resourceful state. You may choose to read a book, relax in a hot bath or go for a walk to calm down, as it is often the simplest of pleasures which help us to relax and funnily enough the only thing usually stopping you from doing these

things is you or your belief around your ability to do them.

During the safety briefing on a plane, why does the airline representative tell you, "in the event of the cabin losing air pressure, when the oxygen masks drop, please ensure you fit your own oxygen mask before you attempt to fit your child's oxygen mask"?

If you run out of oxygen, you won't be in a position to help you child. We can only give our children what *they* need, when our *own* needs are being met.

> ## *Take rest; a field that has rested gives a bountiful crop.*
>
> Ovid

It's often so easy to forget how easy it is to get back to a resourceful state, a state where we can help ourselves and others. We often ignore the opportunities around us, by telling ourselves we're too busy and once again I'd like to remind you of the power of your words and thoughts and if you continue to tell yourself how busy your are, you will continue to create busyness just to prove yourself right.

A more useful mantra to adopt would be something like "I constantly surprise myself how much I am able to achieve each day" or "I always seem to find time to relax and have fun", it's a new instruction for your brain to work on and it will help you to come up with the most wonderful and unexpected solutions to prove you right.

The calmer and nicer you are to yourself and to your kids, the calmer and nicer they'll be to you (remember the hall of a thousand mirrors?)

If you're committed to taking responsibility for yours and your families long term emotional stability, one of the easiest things you can do is start with the things which you have the most control over and I trust you have started to realise you have so much more control over your own thoughts and actions than you do over other peoples and when *you choose to change* the way you think and act, the situations and people around you will start to change for the better. With this new empowerment, I would suggest you choose to make a commitment to yourself today to deliberately and consciously start to gain and maintain a healthy work/life balance, because with balance you get more of the aforementioned resourceful states, more easily and more often.

However, before we continue, may I ask, are you the type of person who keeps a promise?

Great, I knew you were, because on the next exercise I want you to make six promises to yourself which will have the greatest positive affect on your relationship with your children.

Just remember to focus on what you want and make it as specific as possible (i.e. "I promise to sit down and have a family meal together at least five times per week" is more useful than "I promise to eat less take aways", you get the gist.)

I promise

_____

I promise

_____

I promise

_____

I promise

_____

I promise

_____

I promise...

_____

Now I would guess, each promise will require a little bit of action and depending on your personality type, you may wish to break each action down into smaller steps. (i.e. if one of your promises is for you to drink 1.5 litres of still water per day, your first step may be to buy a 1.5 litre water container or to buy a weeks supply of still spring water from you local supermarket.)

Please answer the following question.

My first step for reaching each of my promises is to?

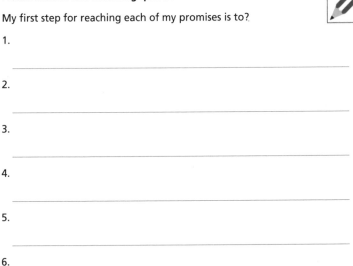

1.

2.

3.

4.

5.

6.

I'm sure you'll agree how important these promises are to enable you to focus on what you actually want, instead of what you don't want. They will also help pull you towards what it is you want, instead of trying to push yourself. Pushing takes effort, being pulled towards your goal is so much easier.

I'm a recovering procrastinator, so I know from experience how hard it can sometimes be to stay focused. I've even been compared to a magpie, who keeps getting distracted by the shiny things around me which have absolutely nothing to do with my main goals in life. So we need to ensure your goals are so compelling you will be naturally drawn towards them.

One thing that really helped me was an interview I heard with Sir Matthew Pincent, the British Olympic rower. He was asked about the fourth gold medal he'd won as part of the four man rowing team at Athens in 2004 and how they'd achieved it considering their poor performance at the world championships the previous year. He explained that the team had got together after the poor results and asked themselves openly and honestly if they really wanted to win the Olympic gold medals the following year and if they did, were they prepared to do whatever it took to reach that goal?

Agreeing that they all did want it to happen, they recognised the fact that they were a four man rowing team, a manager, physiotherapists, trainers, nutritionists, sponsors, boat builders and supporters all offering different opinions and ideas. There was a lot of well meaning input from various sources. Sometimes however this input was contradictory, which resulted in a negative effect on their ability to *stay focused*. So they developed a simple strategy to help them to *make decisions*.

The strategy was in the form of a question. As you know, if you ask yourself great questions, you get great answers. The question they choose was "Will it make the boat go faster?" Simple but fantastically effective. Just imagine for one minute your goal is to win a gold medal at the Olympics and with every decision you make from that moment on, you ask yourself, "will this make the boat go faster?" Should I go to the pub tonight? Should I have a

glass of wine with my lunch? Should I miss training today? Should I ask for more support? Should I go to bed early tonight? Should I eat this chocolate cake?

Well here's a thing you may not be aware of, we all have a primary question that we ask ourselves unconsciously all the time.

So what question do you need to create to help you stay focused on your goal? Or which question could you suggest to help a child stay focused?

If you're a parent with a goal to spend more quality time with your children, you may want to ask yourself the question "What will help me spend more quality time with my children?" or "will this help me spend more quality time with my children?", (i.e. when a friend invites you to have a drink after work for the third time this week, I would imagine your answer would be different if you asked the question first? "will this help me spend more quality time with my children?" or when you're asked if you can help a colleague on a new committee or project, "will this help me spend more quality time with my children?" It's your shout)

If you're a teacher who decides you want to go all out to help make learning more enjoyable for your students, you may choose to ask "how can I get the learning across to my students in a fun way?" or "will this help engage my students?" and I guarantee you'll be more creative in your lesson planning.

Remember, whatever questions you habitually ask yourself will keep getting answered. This is what some of the greatest minds in history have done. They habitually asked themselves a positive question, until they come up with the answer.

Ask yourself great questions and encourage your children to do the same, helping you both to shift from becoming problem solvers to solution seekers.

The pupil with a new desire to pass a certain exam might ask, "what can I do to improve my english grades?"

For Craig who realises that his goal in life is to make his mum proud, would only need to ask "will this make my mum proud?", so when his friends start smoking and offer him a cigarette, instead of asking "will this help me to look older?" or "will this help me to fit in?" He'll ask himself "will this make my mum proud?" and you and I know the answer to that internal question and outcome will be totally different, don't we?

*"Today will never
come again.
Be a blessing.
Be a friend.
Encourage someone.
Take time to care.
Let your words heal,
and not wound."*